# ALDINGTON AND BADSEY VILLAGES IN THE VALE

## A TAPESTRY OF LOCAL HISTORY

# ALDINGTON AND BADSEY VILLAGES IN THE VALE

## A TAPESTRY OF LOCAL HISTORY

EDITED BY
RICHARD PHILLIPS

THE BADSEY SOCIETY

# ALDINGTON AND BADSEY: VILLAGES IN THE VALE
## A TAPESTRY OF LOCAL HISTORY

This first edition published in 2009 by
The Badsey Society, 4 High Street, Badsey, Evesham WR11 7EW, England.
Text copyright © The Badsey Society and the individual authors 2009.
Photographs and illustrations copyright © as indicated.

Printed by Vale Press Limited, Willersey WR12 7RR

ISBN 978 0 954 746940

## THE BADSEY SOCIETY

The Badsey Society was formed at a meeting in the village in February 2002. The Society exists to promote the understanding and study of the villages of Badsey and Aldington, and the surrounding area. For further information see the website – www.badsey.org.uk/society

Other Badsey Society publications –
*A Brief History of Badsey and Aldington,* 2nd edition, T C Sparrow, 2002. 978 0 954 746919.
*Heads and Tales: A History of Badsey Schools,* Maureen Spinks, 2004. 978 0 954 746902.
*Asparagus: Traditional Asparagus Growing in the Vale of Evesham,* 2006, DVD Video.
*Beyond the Blossom: A Survey of a Traditional Plum Orchard on Knowle Hill in the Vale of Evesham,*
   2007, DVD Video.

## COVERS

The covers were designed by Ian Gibson who also painted the view of Badsey from Knowle Hill and of Pear Tree Corner. The front cover shows Ivy House, Aldington from a photo lent by Michael Barnard, a Ministry of Food Ration Book from 1941, a plan of Synehurst under development, a drawing by Mike Lovatt showing the waterwheel at Aldington Mill as imagined, a sketch by Ian Gibson of a 'Devil's toenail' fossil found locally, and a 17th century footstone photographed by Peter Stewart in Badsey churchyard. The back cover shows the seal and signature of William Collett who sold the blacksmith's shop in 1774, and a milk bottle from Harry Robinson's Manor Dairy donated by Roy Page.

# CONTENTS

*For Tony Jerram*
*1937 - 2008*
*First Chairman of the Badsey Society*

# INTRODUCTION

First, a word of explanation for somebody who has picked up a dusty copy of this volume in a second hand bookshop in Kuala Lumpur and is wondering about the title. Aldington and Badsey are two villages in the Vale of Evesham, and that is in the county of Worcestershire, right in the middle of England. We are in a market gardening area famous for its fruit growing and its asparagus. This book is proud to be parochial.

The Badsey Society's third book is different from the other two. This book has nine authors who have each written their own chapter. The result is a lively mixture of interests and styles. Although you may feel the result is more like a patchwork than a tapestry, we hope you will find much here to catch your interest.

As originally planned, this book was to have had two editors. Tony Jerram's sudden death on 3 April 2008 left many of us with a sense of unfinished business. How many of us have since wanted to ask Tony something and then realised we were too late? Tony was able to help in the early planning of the book and his opinions and ideas have certainly shaped its final form. We hope it is a book that Tony would have liked and that it meets his high standards. We are fortunate that Tony had done a lot of work on his own chapter. We do not know how he would have completed it and we have chosen to include it without adding any extra material.

Tony Jerram was the first Chairman of the Badsey Society and his ideas and support drove along many of our activities. Perhaps his biggest contribution is the two videos he made with Will Dallimore. Both *Asparagus* and *Beyond the Blossom* set out to record local customs and practice before they were lost. But if this sounds a little serious, what was produced was entertaining, evocative and full of a gentle pride for local things.

Of course, this book has more than nine authors. As the acknowledgments at the end of each chapter show, many others have helped to bring it together with their information, ideas and illustrations. We hope we have remembered to mention and thank everyone who has contributed. The momentum of the project has been helped by the subscribers who have shown a delightful faith in the publication by buying a copy before it was completed. As editor, I must end with a special thank you to the Badsey Society committee for their help in numerous ways, and especially for Terry Sparrow whose enlightened comments have improved every chapter.

Richard Phillips, 2009
Badsey, Worcestershire

*A familiar sight in 2008 for all visitors to Badsey: David Caswell and the blacksmith's shop, occupied by his family for nearly one hundred years.*

*David Caswell at work in 2002.*

# 1

# THE VILLAGE BLACKSMITH

## MAUREEN SPINKS

The year 2009 is a special date in the history of Badsey blacksmiths. This is the year in which David Caswell, the current blacksmith, celebrates the centenary of his family's blacksmithing business. As far as David is concerned, 14th February is the key date, exactly a hundred years since his grandfather arrived in the village. David has always said he would be sure to light a fire in the forge, invite in his friends, and have a gossip, as blacksmiths through the ages have been wont to do.

The village blacksmith is indeed an iconic figure in English history and literature. Henry Wadsworth Longfellow in his poem *The Village Blacksmith* provides a template for our view of the 19th century blacksmith: "a mighty man is he, with large and sinewy hands; and the muscles of his brawny arms are strong as iron bands" who "looks the whole world in the face, for he owes not any man." Charles Dickens in *Great Expectations* portrays Joe Gargery, the village blacksmith, as a symbol of happiness and contentment and a role model for young Pip, the hero of the novel.

The word *blacksmith* refers to iron, which was known as the *black* metal, and *smith,* meaning a smiter of metal. Blacksmithing dates back to the Iron Age when man first began making tools from iron and discovered that a certain type of rock yielded iron when heated by the coals of a very hot campfire. By hammering it into shape before it cooled, he could make a sword or other implements. It was not until the 9th century that the blacksmith began horseshoeing and became a prominent figure in the town or village, a position that lasted until the invention of the automobile. The surname of Smith is the commonest in the United Kingdom, reflecting how important a trade it was when surnames began a few centuries ago.

We are lucky still to have a blacksmith in Badsey. For so many villages, the smithy is a thing of the past. But the Caswells are not the only family with a long tradition of blacksmithing in our village. There were the Birds who were blacksmiths for 75 years and the Oldakers for a century, as well as several other individuals and countless unnamed people before them, who have all played their part to a greater or lesser degree in the honourable trade of blacksmithing in the village.

The familiar figure of David Caswell leaning over the door at his premises lends an air of permanence to the situation. Just as the name Caswell is taken to be synonymous with the village blacksmith, most people assume that the forge has always been there and always will be, but there have been at least three other locations for the forge since the late 17th century.

We are coming to the end of an era as 69-year-old David, the third and last generation of blacksmiths in his family, is slowly winding down towards retirement and there is no one to follow. Will Badsey go the way of most other villages in the Vale, where the blacksmith and his forge are consigned to the history books? The future is unknown, but we can look back on the past to find out more about the people who occupied this pivotal role in the village community.

## James and Henry Bird

Undoubtedly there were blacksmiths in Badsey since time immemorial, but the first known one was James Bird. James, born at Bretforton in 1668, plied his trade right in the heart of Badsey, close to the church. His forge no longer exists, but it was just a short distance from the present-day forge, situated in what is now part of the churchyard, to the north of the lychgate in Chapel Street.

James Bird married Margery Smith in the 1690s and probably opened the forge on his move to Badsey. The couple were certainly living in Badsey by 1695 when their daughter Ann was baptised. Sadly, Margery died a few months after her daughter's birth and Ann died at the age of two. James then married Anne Phipps at Badsey in 1697. James and Anne had four sons and two daughters. It was Henry, the fourth child and eldest surviving son, who followed his father into the blacksmith's business after James' death in 1728.

What type of work would James and Henry Bird have done and what would the forge have been like? Most blacksmiths' shops were small and poorly lit. The main tools were a forge and bellows, an anvil, hammers, and a small selection of files and tongs. Traditionally, we think of the blacksmith as a farrier, a person who shod horses, but many trades were dependent on him. He was at times a wheelwright, carpenter, veterinarian, and dentist, among other things. Most blacksmiths were toolmakers, making and repairing tools for the farmer such as hoes and shovels, tools for women including cooking, sewing, and household tools, tools for hunting and tools for industry and other trades, including those for the blacksmith himself. The blacksmith was held in high esteem but, for all his skill and talents, he was often considered a simple, uneducated man who seemed more comfortable spending his day inside his hellish forge than anywhere else.

Whether or not the forge had been built for James Bird is not known, but a lease drawn up many years later in 1774, described it as "All that messuage or tenement with the stable, blacksmith's shop, yard and garden, thereunto belonging situate standing and being in Badsey aforesaid in the said county of Worcester, formerly occupied by James Bird and afterwards by Henry Bird his son."[1]

Henry Bird, who had been born in 1705, was a young man of 23 when he inherited the business in 1728. He did not marry until he was about 40 and, like today's blacksmith, he had four daughters, although two daughters pre-deceased him. By the time of Henry's death in 1774, he had fulfilled the role of 'the village blacksmith' for nearly 50 years.

From his will[2] of 1772, it seems that Henry's business had been successful, as he had property in both Badsey and Little Comberton to pass on. Henry had written the will himself and not got witnesses, so Thomas Cottrell and Joseph Simpson, who were near neighbours and often transacted business with him, had to testify that it was definitely his handwriting.

By the terms of the will, Henry's two surviving daughters, Mary and Elizabeth, were given legacies of money, but it was his son-in-law, William Collett, and grandson, William, who received the bulk of the estate. William Collett was the widower of Henry's daughter, Nancy, who had died in 1770, one month after giving birth to baby William. William Collett senior received Henry's estate at Little Comberton and his house and buildings in Badsey, with William Collett junior to inherit the estate and receive £200 on reaching the age of 21.

In April 1774, just over two months after his father-in-law's death, William Collett sold the blacksmith's shop, yard and garden, with the cottage and stable for £50 to Richard Oldaker. This sale possibly enabled William to buy The Firs (today's 27 High Street) where he was living at the time of the passing of the Badsey Enclosure Act of 1812. After just over three-quarters of a century with the Birds as blacksmiths, a new era in Badsey blacksmithing was about to take place when the Oldaker family began a hundred year association with the trade in Badsey.

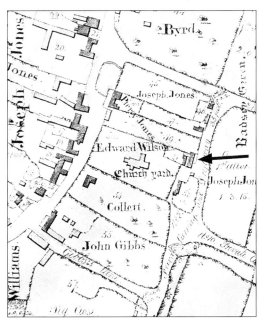

*The Badsey Enclosure Map of 1812 shows the location of the blacksmith's owned by Samuel Oldaker.*

*The former blacksmith's cottage, about 1913, some 40 years after it had ceased being a blacksmith's. Almost the last people to occupy the cottage were the Roberts family who lived there from 1906 to 1924. Here you can see Charlie, George, Bessie and Nelly Roberts. The cottage eventually fell into ruin, becoming just a pile of stones overgrown with brambles, before being finally pulled down in the late 1940s for the churchyard extension.*

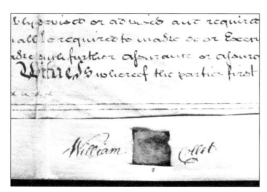

*The seal and signature of William Collett. In 1774, he sold the blacksmith's shop and cottage for £50 to Richard Oldaker.*

## The Oldakers

Richard Oldaker, who bought the business in 1774, had been born at Wickhamford in 1737, the fifth of eight children of Thomas and Mary Oldaker. In the early 1750s, the Oldakers moved from Wickhamford to Badsey; Thomas' occupation is unknown.

Richard was 37 when he took over the blacksmith's business. He had presumably been apprenticed to Henry Bird and learnt his skills under an experienced smith. Richard's buying of the business coincided with the raising of a growing family. He had married Mary Wheatley at Weston Subedge in March 1772. They had two sons and five daughters born between 1772 and 1790, two of the daughters dying in childhood.

Richard died in 1796 at the age of 59. Two years after his death, Richard's widow, Mary, married widower Charles Simpson, ending her days in Evesham in 1844. Richard and Mary's eldest daughter, Mary, also married a Charles Simpson in 1793 (the son of the other Charles). It was through the Simpson connection that, many years later, Richard and Mary's great-grandson, John Cornelius Simpson, tried to rescue the, by then, ailing business.

After Richard's death, his eldest son, Samuel Oldaker, took over the business. Samuel had been born in 1775 and was not quite 21 when his father died. Samuel married Elizabeth Need at Sedgeberrow in 1798 and they had three children, Mary Ann, Elizabeth and Richard. Samuel ran the business for 45 years until his death in 1839, caused by 'decay of nature'.

Samuel was probably the very epitome of 'the village blacksmith', fortunate to practise his trade at a time when blacksmiths were still in great demand. Following the Enclosure Act of 1812, farms at Claybrook and Bowers Hill had been created, which generated more work. Tractors would not replace horsepower for another century, and so there were always plenty of horses to be shod. When Samuel died in 1839 at the age of 64, he obviously felt that he had left the business in a sound shape for his widow and then his son and grandson to inherit.

Under the terms of Samuel's will[3] of 1839, Charles Drury, a farmer, and Edward Laugher Blew, a baker, both of Badsey, had been appointed trustees. By now there were two cottages: one connected to the blacksmith's shop and a separate one occupied by Giles Dobbins. Samuel's trustees held the premises in trust for his widow, Elizabeth, for her lifetime, "to have the sole use and enjoyment of my said household furniture and effects for her life and also the use of my stock in trade, tools and implements of trade to carry on my said trade of a blacksmith if she should think proper for her own use and benefit". Within 12 months of the death of Elizabeth, £45 was to be paid to each of his daughters, Mary and Elizabeth, and his son, Richard, was to have the rents and profits from the tenements and blacksmith's shop for his lifetime. On Elizabeth's death, all the household furniture and effects were to be equally divided between the three children. His tools and implements of trade were, on the death of his wife, to go to his son, Richard, and after his death, to his grandson, Richard and any other children of his son, Richard.

Though not traditionally considered a woman's job, there have been women blacksmiths at least since the Middle Ages. Married women often assisted their husbands in their trades and sometimes practised the trade when their husbands were away, so it was not unusual that Samuel would expect Elizabeth to carry on in the family business if she wanted to. However, it seems that Elizabeth, although she remained living at the cottage attached to the blacksmith's shop for the rest of her life, passed over the reins to her son, Richard, whilst she and her unmarried daughter, Mary Ann, worked as glove makers.

When Richard assumed the role of the village blacksmith, life was not easy for him. His first wife,

Elizabeth Knight, had died in 1837 after just two years of marriage leaving him with a baby son, Richard. Young Richard was brought up by his grandmother at the blacksmith's cottage, whilst Richard senior lived elsewhere in the village. Richard married again in 1845 to Louisa Berrington from Fladbury and they had six children. They lived on Bakers Lane (now School Lane), on the corner with the High Street, just a few minutes' walk from his mother and sister and the blacksmith's shop.

Tragedy struck in 1855 when the younger Richard died of consumption aged 19. By the terms of his grandfather's will, young Richard had been due to inherit the tools of trade of his grandfather's blacksmith business after his grandmother and father's death, but he died before either of them. Richard, however, had not followed his father into the blacksmith's trade; instead, he was working as a carpenter. Young Richard's death was followed in 1860 by the death of his father who died of dropsy. Elizabeth Oldaker thus outlived both her son and grandson.

In the final years of her life, Elizabeth had to pick up the blacksmithing trade again. The 1861 census reveals that both 85-year-old Elizabeth and 60-year-old Mary Ann were working as blacksmiths. Not only were their personal circumstances difficult, but the trade of blacksmithing was changing. In Dickens' *Great Expectations,* written in 1860, the blacksmith was still an important figure in the community but was on the brink of extinction because of the turn towards industrialism. It could not have been easy for them.

At the same time that the two elderly women were desperately trying to keep the business together, Richard's widow, Louisa, was staying in Aston with her brother-in-law, John Cornelius Simpson, the widowed husband of her sister, Nancy. She had taken two of her children with her,

14-year-old Nancy and the youngest, four-year-old John, leaving three of her children behind in Badsey. There was also a family connection in another way. John Simpson was the great-grandson of Richard Oldaker, the first Oldaker to buy the business, and the first cousin-once-removed of her dead husband. Just two months later, John and Louisa married at the Church of St Peter and St Paul, Aston. Was it a marriage of convenience? John had started out as a whitesmith, a person who works with 'white' or light-coloured metals such as tin and pewter, but was now an agricultural implement maker employing eight people. Did Louisa hope that by going to Aston she could persuade John to assist in the business? While blacksmiths work mostly with hot metal, whitesmiths do the majority of their work on cold metal (although they might use a forge to shape their raw materials), but presumably John had acquired sufficient skills to try and keep the blacksmith's business going.

Elizabeth Oldaker died at Badsey in 1866, aged 90, without making a will. The following year, the elderly trustees of Samuel Oldaker's will (81-year-old Charles Drury and 75-year-old Edward Laugher Blew) appointed brothers, John Redgrave, a solicitor, and Elisha Redgrave, an auctioneer, as the new trustees. At the time of the appointment in July 1867, Mary Oldaker had ceased living at the blacksmith's cottage and John Cornelius Simpson was named as being in occupation. Louisa, the widow of Richard Oldaker and now married to John

*The 1861 census of Badsey gives the occupation of 85-year-old Elizabeth Oldaker (spelt incorrectly on the census form as Oldacre) and her 60-year-old daughter, Mary Ann, as blacksmith. Elizabeth's other daughter, Elizabeth Silvester, was also staying. (Ref RG9/2102, f 81, p 18.)*

| Name and Surname of each Person | Relation to Head of Family | Condition | Age of Males \| Females | Rank, Profession, or Occupation | Where Born | Wh Blind, and-1 |
|---|---|---|---|---|---|---|
| Elizabeth Oldacre | Head | Wid | 85 | Blacksmith | Do Sedgeborough | |
| Mary Ann do | Daur | Un | 60 | do | Do Badsey | |
| Elizabeth Silvester | Daur | Mar | 50 | | Do do | |
| Elizabeth Gardner | Border | Un | 8 | | Warwickshire Birmingham | |
| Joseph Clements | Lodger | Un | 50 | Tailor | Gloucestershire Ashton Under Hill | |

Cornelius Simpson, had obviously been successful in getting him to come to Badsey to try and revive the ailing business. Under the terms of Samuel Oldaker's will of 1839, Messrs Redgrave needed to pay £45 to each of Samuel Oldaker's daughters, so they mortgaged the property to John Unett for £120.

The years following are rather a mystery. By the time of the 1871 census, neither John nor Louisa was living in Badsey. Louisa had reverted to the name of Oldaker and was to be found living at 96 Great Hampton Street, Birmingham, and was described as an 'eating house keeper'. Also living there were her son John Oldaker and her daughter Louisa Steers with her baby son. Meanwhile, John Cornelius Simpson's whereabouts are unknown. His 13-year-old youngest son, also called John Cornelius, was staying with a cousin and her husband, but neither John senior, nor the rest of his family, was anywhere to be seen in the United Kingdom census.

Back in Badsey, the financial situation had not improved. At the end of 1873, John Redgrave redeemed the mortgage for £120 out of his own money. By the terms of Samuel Oldaker's will, all the grandchildren were to inherit the property equally (by this time, it was inheriting the considerable debts). It is possible that the only grandchild surviving was John Oldaker, the youngest grandchild, who attained the age of 21 on 1st November 1877. He was unable to pay back John Redgrave the money owing to him.

It was at this point that John Oldaker's employer came to the rescue. In 1871, John had been living with his mother and married sister, Louisa, in Birmingham, but he later moved to the USA, where he worked as groom for Alfred Berrington of Chicago. Alfred was a hotel keeper and lived at 22 Lake Street, Chicago but, more importantly, he was also John's cousin, some 17 years his senior. On 29th September 1877, when both John Oldaker and Alfred Berrington were temporarily back in Evesham, Alfred bought the blacksmith's shop and cottages.

A month later, on 27th October 1877, the property was sold at public auction for £160 to Mr Thomas Walter Green of Evesham:

> "All that messuage or tenement with the Blacksmith's shop, land and premises thereto belonging situate in Badsey in the County of Worcester, late in the occupation of Mary Oldaker, afterwards of John Cornelius Simpson, late of David Walker and then void, And also all that cottage or tenement with the land and appurtenances thereto belonging situate adjoining the hereditaments described at Badsey aforesaid, formerly in the occupation of Giles Dobbins, afterwards of Oliver Rogers and then void, And all other of any the hereditaments at Badsey aforesaid devised by the said Samuel Oldaker deceased and comprised in the thereinbefore recited Indentures."

The business of blacksmithing had not been conducted on the premises for some years. After the sale, the two cottages were let out to tenants and the forge was just used as an outhouse. It was the end of an era for the Oldakers after having owned the business for a century.

## Samuel Godden, William Moore, Charles Collett

Parish records for the 1850s and early 1860s give evidence of other people with the occupation of blacksmith living in the village. These were probably people brought in by the Oldaker family to assist with their ailing business.

One such person was Samuel Godden who was living and working in Badsey by 1852. Born in South Petherton, Somerset, in about 1808, he had moved to Bengeworth with his first wife in the 1830s, where he worked as a blacksmith. Following the death of his wife and three sons, leaving him with two young children, Samuel married Charlotte Knight of Badsey in 1851. They remained in Badsey until the early 1860s. By 1871, Samuel Godden and family were back in Bengeworth, Samuel still working as a blacksmith.

In the mid 1850s, William Coldicott Moore came to assist. He was born at Long Marston, Gloucestershire, about 1837 and married Ann Drinkwater at Badsey in 1857; they had a son, George Drinkwater Moore in 1859. They had gone from Badsey by 1860 when their daughter, Ellen was born. William spent the rest of his life working as a blacksmith, firstly at North Littleton, then at Campden and then at South Littleton.

By 1861, 23-year-old Charles Collett was working as a blacksmith in Badsey. Charles had been born in Willersey, but he and his wife, Victoria, had been living in Cleeve Prior. His younger brother, William, had recently moved to Badsey, working as a servant at The Royal Oak, but possibly it was through Elizabeth Sylvester (daughter of Samuel and Elizabeth Oldaker), who had lived at Cleeve Prior, that he got the job. Charles and Victoria and their two young sons lived at The Leys, the same group of cottages where the Oldaker children (Elizabeth Sylvester's nieces and nephews) were living in 1861. Charles remained in Badsey for two to three years, a daughter Catherine being baptised in Badsey church in 1863. By 1865, they had moved to Welford on Avon where Charles gained employment as blacksmith before finishing his days in Cleeve Prior, again as a blacksmith.

## The new blacksmith's shop; Francis Thistle

Whilst the Oldaker business was on the wane, another blacksmith's shop opened up in the 1860s in Badsey on the High Street, in one of the outbuildings on land next to Hollywood Villa. This is the house known today as Greystones, 10A High Street, but many older residents of the village remember it as being a butcher's shop in the mid 20th century.

The premises, together with the neighbouring Hollywood Villa (which was rebuilt in 1996), had been owned by the absentee Wilson family (very distant relatives of the Wilsons of the Manor House) in the early part of the 19th century. In July 1842, William George Wilson of Portsmouth sold it to James Ashwin of Bretforton who, later in the year, sold it to Edward Appelbee of Harrington House. The sale comprised "All that messuage tenement or farm house with the wheelwright's shop, dovecote, outhouses and other outbuildings homestead and garden thereto belonging … ".[4]

There is no evidence from census returns that the wheelwright's shop was being used. Hollywood Villa was let out to tenants who worked as agricultural labourers and had no specialist craft and there were no wheelwrights in the village in the latter part of the 19th century. A date-stone in the wall outside the present-day Greystones has the date of 1860 or 1863 (the inscription is difficult to read), so probably that was the year when Mrs Elizabeth Appelbee, Edward's widow, decided to revamp the premises.

According to today's blacksmith, David Caswell, the building was purpose-built as a blacksmith's. In David's youth it had become a butcher's shop run by Elgar Hartwell. Although he never knew it as a blacksmith's, he recalls that evidence of its previous existence was visible right up until its conversion to residential accommodation in 1975. At the rear was an open archway known as the *penthouse* where

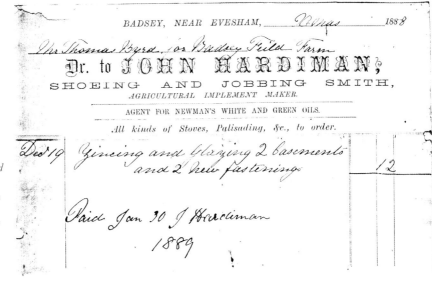

An 1888 invoice issued by John Hardiman to Thomas Byrd for work done at Badsey Field Farm for "zincing and glazing two casements and two new fastenings".

*Above: Greystones, 10A High Street, converted to residential accommodation in 1975, from the building which housed the blacksmith's forge in the late 19th century.*

*Below: Helen Stanton (née Hartwell) with relatives, standing outside the same building in June 1958. For several decades in the 20th century, it was used as a butcher's shop by her parents, Elgar and Helen Hartwell.*

*Bottom picture: The present-day blacksmith, David Caswell, shows home-owners, Steve Entwistle and Gaynor Heath, where the open archway known as the Penthouse used to be, where the horses stood to be shod.*

the horses stood to be shod, kept away from the forge. The actual forge was between the arch and the shop.

Certainly by the late 1860s, Mrs Appelbee was advertising her premises for use as a wheelwright's shop or blacksmith. The added attraction was that the neighbouring Hollywood Villa was also available to rent. Francis Thistle, born about 1837 in Flitcham, Norfolk, and his wife and two children arrived to take up the post. Francis and his wife, Pleasance, had moved from Norfolk to Whitbourne, Herefordshire around 1860, and then to Ombersley, Worcestershire in about 1865. By 1871 Francis and Pleasance and three children were settled in Hollywood Villa.

In 1873, the Thistle family, by now with another child, decided to seek their fortune in the United States of America. Elizabeth Appelbee advertised in The Evesham Journal[5] for a new tenant.

> BLACKSMITHS AND WHEELWRIGHTS, BADSEY - To be let, and entered upon at Lady Day next, suitable premises for carrying on the above trades, comprising House (to which is attached a small Grocery business), Two Gardens, Shops for Blacksmith (two forges), and Wheelwright or Carpenter, Stable, Timber Yard, etc, etc. Apply to Mrs Appelbee, Badsey.

The Thistles departed for America where they were to be found, at the time of the 1880 American census, living at Osage, Allen, Kansas. Francis, and his eldest son, William, were both employed as blacksmiths.

## John Hardiman, William Moore

In 1871, 18-year-old John Hardiman was Francis Thistle's apprentice. John had been born in Winchcombe in 1853, but his mother, Emma Higgins, was from Badsey, and he had relatives in the village. John Hardiman took over from Francis Thistle, presumably in 1873, and remained as the blacksmith in the village until 1891.

John married Mary Anne Turner of Fladbury in 1874. Their first-born son, John, died in 1878 at the age of two. Three months later, Mary Ann was born, followed by Fanny Maria in 1881 and Thomas Henry in 1890. For most of their time in Badsey, they lived in Hollywood Villa although, at the time

# PARTICULARS.

## The Property will be offered in the following Lots :—

LOT 1.—All that very Desirable

# STONE-BUILT RESIDENCE,

Containing Five Bedrooms, Attics, Dining and Drawing-rooms, Back and Front Kitchens, Pantry, and usual Offices, with the Pleasure and Kitchen Gardens, newly-erected Stables, Coachhouse, large Barn, and Sheds, also the adjoining STONE-BUILT COTTAGE, SHOEING FORGE, Warehouse and Out-offices.

Also all that

# FINE ORCHARD

At the rear of the above Premises, running down to the Brook. The whole of this Lot contains 3A. 1R. 14P., and is in the several occupations of Mr. S. Johns and Messrs. Moore, Robbins, and Addis, at an estimated rent of £52 per annum.

This Lot (which is numbered 120, 125, and 126 on Plan) has a frontage of about 70 yards to the Main Street in Badsey, and has two double gate entrances, rendering it well adapted for being divided into separate lots for Building Sites. Land Tax on this Lot, 18s. 6d.

LOT 2.—A very Valuable and

# WELL-FRUITED PASTURE ORCHARD

Facing the last Lot and fronting the Main Street at Badsey aforesaid, and containing 1A. 0R. 13P. (No. 138 on Plan.)

of the 1881 census, they were living elsewhere, as the house was occupied by a farm bailiff who had come to look after the estate following the recent death of Elizabeth Appelbee.

Elizabeth Appelbee died in 1880. It took another 11 years after Elizabeth's death before the Appelbee estate was sold, complicated by the fact that both Elizabeth's children had pre-deceased her. Hollywood Villa and the adjoining blacksmith's shop were sold as part of the Harrington House estate by the trustees of the will of Thomas Appelbee and his sister, Mrs William Gibbs, at a sale[6] at the King's Head Hotel, Evesham, on 6th July 1891. They were described as "the adjoining stone-built cottage, shoeing forge, warehouse and out-offices" and were sold in Lot 1, together with Harrington House and the orchard at the rear, to Arthur Edward Jones of Badsey.

John Hardiman had left the village three months before the sale. Shortly before census night on 5th April 1891, he had taken up a position as blacksmith in the High Street, Blockley. He ended his days in Worcester in 1907 where he had gone to work in an iron foundry.

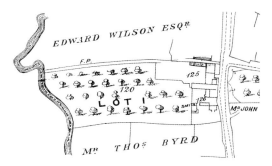

*The blacksmith's forge was sold as part of Lot 1 by the trustees of the Appelbee estate. The other buildings referred to are Harrington House and Hollywood Villa*

The end of the 19th century and the start of the 20th century appear to have been a lean time for the blacksmith industry in Badsey. It is most likely that the people of Badsey were served by a series of short-term blacksmiths. In 1892, a blacksmith named William Moore (possibly a distant relative of the William Moore who was a blacksmith in Badsey for a few years in the 1850s), resided in the parish for a short time when his son, Walter Henry, was baptised. He lived at Hollywood Villa, so the forge was obviously still in use for a time in the 1890s. By 1901, he had moved to Offenham where he worked as a painter and glazier. No one with the occupation of blacksmith was listed in the 1901 Badsey census.

In 1921, Arthur Jones sold "All that cottage called or known as Hollywood Villa (formerly occupied as two tenements) and the warehouse outbuildings … together with the stable and loft over the shoeing forge and the shed adjoining the said shoeing forge"[7], plus Harrington House and the orchard, to Edward Johns, whose family had been tenants at Harrington House since the late 1880s. It is unlikely that it had been used as a blacksmith's forge for some time and, shortly after the Johns family acquired the property, it was turned into a butcher's shop.

## Aldington

During the 19th century, blacksmith's premises existed in Aldington, but there was no permanent blacksmith, certainly at least by the second half of the century. The Aldington Enclosure Commissioners[8] in their Award Schedules of 1808 make reference to a blacksmith's shop:

"Also all that Blacksmith's Shop and part House situate in or near the Village of Aldington aforesaid together with the site thereof, bounded on the West and North by the Allotment Awarded to the said George Day for late Brookes's, on the East by a Cottage Garden belonging to the said George Day, and on the South by Pitwell Road aforesaid, the said Messuage, Garden, Blacksmith's Shop and part House being Awarded as aforesaid by the said Commissioners by and with the consent of the said Edward Laugher testified by his signing and sealing these presents."

This blacksmith's shop is thought to have been approximately where the present-day house called Middlebank is situated on Main Street. At the beginning of the 19th century, it had belonged to Edward Laugher. George Day, Lord of the Manor and owner of Aldington Farm since 1805, owned all the surrounding land. In 1808, when the Aldington Enclosure Commissioners made their awards, George Day was allotted Edward Laugher's property as compensation for other land which had been redistributed. On 6th October 1808, just two days after the Enclosure Awards, George Day sold this plot of land, together with all the estate bought from Lord Foley in 1805, to James Ashwin of Bretforton.

*Map of 1883 showing the location of the smithy in Aldington.*

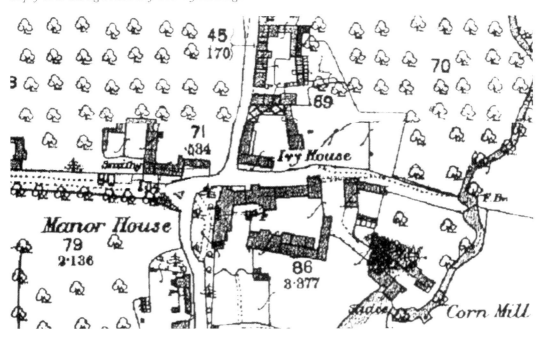

Later in the century (and probably soon after the Ashwins acquired the manorial estate), the blacksmith's shop was relocated closer to the Manor, in a location by the old Cider Mill and Corner Cottage. Parish records and census returns make no reference to a blacksmith in Aldington, so it would appear that there was no resident blacksmith. This is confirmed by Arthur Savory, the tenant farmer at Aldington Manor from 1873-1902, who wrote[9]:

> "Our blacksmith came twice a week to the village when work was still plentiful in the early days of my farming, and I was not yet the only practical farmer in the place. I need not describe the forge: it has been sung by Longfellow, made music of by Handel, and painted by Morland; everybody knows its gleaming red-hot iron, its cascades of sparks, and the melodious clank of the heavy hammer as it falls upon the impressionable metal. In all pursuits which entail the use of an open fire at night, its fascination attracts both busy and idle villagers, and more especially in winter it becomes a centre for local gossip. At that season, the time-honoured gossip corner, close to the Manor gate, was deserted for the warmth and action of the forge."

The blacksmith to whom he was referring was most likely John Hardiman of Badsey. The Aldington smithy has not been used in living memory. It is believed that it ceased operation in the early 20th century.

### The Willersey Road Smithy; Thomas King

At the beginning of the 20th century, a new smithy was built in Badsey. In 1904, John Idiens & Sons Limited had acquired land off Willersey Road called The Stockey. Work began in 1905 to erect 14 cottages and a smithy, which were available for occupation by 1906. In March 1906, Thomas King came as the new blacksmith. In 1901 he had been a blacksmith in Broadway, followed by a time at Willersey. Sadly, within two months of moving to Badsey, Thomas' fourth child, six-year-old Frederick, died in a diphtheria epidemic which spread through the village. According to the school registers, the family left the village in October 1909.

Since the erection of the smithy and cottages in 1906, John Idiens & Sons Limited had been drawing

*Lisbon House, Willersey Road, on the site of a smithy which had been erected in the early 20th century.*

the rents. However, the company ran into financial difficulties and the bank, declaring themselves as the beneficial owners, put the cottages and the piece of land 'with the cement erection of a Smithy standing thereon' up for sale in 1911.

But the days of the smithy on Willersey Road were numbered because a new forge had recently been opened on Chapel Street. In the mid 20th century the Willersey Road building was used as a fertiliser store and garage by Tom Bennett who owned the land. It was pulled down in the early 1960s to make way for a new dwelling house, Lisbon House, No. 62 Willersey Road.

### The Chapel Street Forge; the Caswells

Shortly before Thomas King left Badsey, a young man from Bretforton arrived whose family were to remain as blacksmiths in Badsey for the next hundred years. It was on 14th February 1909 that the Caswell family began their long association with Badsey and with the premises on Chapel Street, which are so well-known to people all over the Vale.

Frank Caswell, a man in his mid-twenties and soon to become a father, had been born at Stretton on Fosse in 1883, one of five children of Ernest and Julia Caswell. At the time of the 1901 census, he had been lodging in West Bromwich, working as a shoeing smith. Some time after this he moved to the Vale where he met his bride-to-be, Charlotte Matilda Robbins. Frank and Charlotte were wed at St Leonard's Church, Bretforton in 1908.

The property which Frank Caswell rented, described as 'the barn', had been a blacksmith's shop for about two years before he took it on, but it was disused. For most of the 19th century, it had been owned by the Bishop family. William Bishop, who owned the cottage and workshop at the time of the Badsey Enclosure Act of 1812 was a shoemaker by trade. He built an extension to his workshop in 1830 (it is still possible to see 'WB 1830' carved faintly into the red-brick wall to the right of the forge entrance) and it was this extension which proved ideal for the blacksmith's forge.

An important event occurred just over a month after their move to Badsey when Frank and Charlotte's son, Richard Henry Caswell (Dick), was born on 20th March 1909. After leaving school in 1922, Dick became apprenticed to his father. Frank Caswell's business was growing in Badsey and, when the opportunity arose in 1928, he bought the cottage and blacksmith's shop from Mr Bishop for £400. Frank also operated a workshop in Bretforton which he and Dick opened two days a week. Bretforton was more of a farming village than

*The blacksmith's shop in Chapel Street, 1927; Frank Caswell and his son, Dick, are about to repair a plough.*

Badsey, and so there were teams of cart-horses to be shod. In Badsey, the farrier side of the business was dealing with market gardeners' cobs, plus looking after the horses belonging to the two bakeries.

The Bretforton business closed in the 1930s, which was at the time when Frank changed direction and became a market gardener, leaving Dick to carry on the business by himself until, many years later, his son David was able to join him. When Frank died in 1962 the Parish Magazine[10] contained the following appreciation of his life:

"Frank Caswell will be sadly missed. He was a great lover of past traditions, and delighted to tell stories about the old days. But he was not just a talker about these things. We in Badsey have cause to be thankful that Frank came from Bretforton over 50 years ago to set up his forge in our village and maintain the very highest traditions of the blacksmith's craft. He courageously held on at a time when smiths all over the country were going out of business. Furthermore he passed on his skill and enthusiasm to the second and third generations. Son and grandson carry on his work, and Badsey forge is always busy, for it has a great reputation throughout the south-west midlands. We are

*The Bishop of Worcester visited the Caswells' forge in August 1962. Dick Caswell and his son David met the bishop, Dr L M Charles-Edwards who was shown market gardening tools made there.*

very proud of our smithy, and we thank God for our old blacksmith, praying that his soul may find refreshment and peace. Our warm sympathy to Mrs Caswell and the family. We are so glad that Mrs David Caswell has been safely delivered of twins."

At the time when the village blacksmith was in decline throughout most of the country, trade for the Caswells flourished during the heyday of market gardening. It was Dick who in the 1930s made the first sprout net holder, which soon became a familiar device in Vale market gardens. A sprout net holder is a hoop of iron which stands on the floor, with struts that rise to another, unfinished hoop, from which the sprout net hangs. The Caswells also became famous as being the makers of the Evesham hoe and asparagus knife. In the first half of the 20th century, when the production of asparagus was at its height, a Caswell knife was a necessity with its thin, razor-sharp blade which sliced the vegetable away at the root under the ground.

When tractors began to replace horses on the farms and market gardens, the farrier side of the blacksmith's job became less important. The Wolseley Merry Tiller (a small 'walking tractor') was an important invention of the 1950s. By the early 1960s, there was hardly a market gardener in the Vale who did not have one and the Caswells were kept busy making all the tools which went with it

as it quickly became established that their custom made tools were superior to the ones supplied by the company.

Although there were not many farm horses to shoe, people would bring their hunters from miles around to have them shod in Badsey. Many 20th century farriers bought their horseshoes ready-made, but not Dick Caswell. He preferred to make them himself as it was cheaper and he felt they were of better quality. So, all winter was spent shoeing hunters and all spring and summer spent making tools.

One person who assisted Dick Caswell from time to time was Frank Wheeler. Frank worked as a blacksmith for two or three different companies in Evesham, but loved to spend time in the forge at Badsey. He was also tenant of a piece of land on the way to Bowers Hill. Whilst he did some market gardening, his main love was blacksmithing and it was on this ground in a wooden shed that he had a small anvil and hand-pumped forge where he would shoe the odd horse. In an obituary in the Parish Magazine of April 1969, Frank was described as "a good craftsman of the old school: a blacksmith and wheelwright".

Dick Caswell carried on working until he was 79. He died in 1992, knowing that the business, which his father had started back in 1909, was safe in the hands of his son. Following in his father's footsteps, David Caswell, after leaving Prince Henry's Grammar School, had joined his father in the family business in 1955. He also undertook a part-time five-year apprentice's course at Hereford College and became a skilled metal work and agricultural engineer and a qualified gas and electric welder. Unlike his father and grandfather before him, the farrier's work made up only half of his business.

*An asparagus knife made by the Caswells.*

*This page and opposite: A series of pictures from June 2002 showing David Caswell in his forge. Photos by Terry J Morgan of Chipping Campden with thanks to Sarah Bent.*

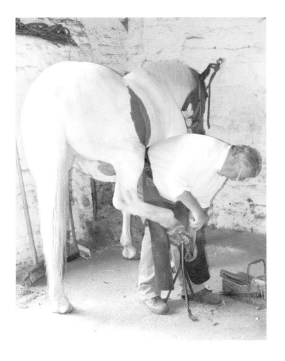

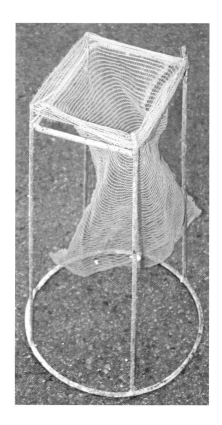

*Above: The Wolseley Merry Tiller. This model of walking tractor was popular with market gardeners in the 1960s. The Caswells made tools that fitted to it. This 2008 photo shows David Caswell and market gardener Mike Hewlett who both still own Merry Tillers.*

*Above right: A sprout net holder designed and made by the Caswells. The sprout picker put the holder between two rows of sprouts. After stripping the sprouts from two plants on each side and putting them in the net, the holder was moved forward. When the net was full, it was weighed and the contents adjusted to reach the correct weight. The net was then tied ready to send to market. The next net was then fitted to the holder. Terry Sparrow recalls that the most accomplished pickers could fill as many as one hundred nets in a day.*

Now an old-age pensioner, David Caswell has not shod a horse for two years. He does, however, still dabble in a bit of blacksmithing, but these days he might just as easily be asked to make a candlestick or a curtain rail as to make an agricultural implement. He continues to watch the comings and goings of village life from his forge, which forms a regular meeting-place each morning for his friends.

But it is his skills as a raconteur that have been uppermost in the last few years. He is on the tourist circuit for visitors to the Vale and entertains holidaymakers who have cycled from Dumbleton Hall to see the blacksmith's forge which has changed very little since David's grandfather's day. Outside of a museum, you would be hard-pushed to find a traditional smithy such as the one we have in Badsey. A few years ago, his 'Tales from the Forge' was a popular monthly column in The Vale Magazine.

What of the future of the blacksmith industry in Badsey? David Caswell's intention has always been to carry on until 2009, to celebrate the centenary of his family setting up business in the village. None of his four daughters has felt inclined to follow in his footsteps and the grandchildren are still at school. Sadly, we seem to be coming to the end of an era. After David Caswell, will there be anyone else to take on the role of the village blacksmith in the last-remaining traditional forge in the Vale? The ring of the hammer on an anvil was once a familiar sound in every village, where the blacksmith was a vital part of the community, but sadly this may soon be a sound of the past.

# Tales from the Forge

## Dying to see you

BLACKSMITH David Caswell offers another tale from the forge. He has fond memories of his granny Lottie and her friend Elsie who both enjoyed poor health.

"Elsie used to visit us every Tuesday afternoon at Forge Cottage," recalls David, "and they would always try to out-do each other about who felt the worst!

"I remember my grandad saying, "'Er's here again. If your granny was having a babby old Else would be having twins!'" One day David overheard Elsie. "Oh my God Lottie, I be bad you. You know this morning when I woke up I felt that bad I thought I was dying." David's granny replied, "I be just the same. I don't know what to do with meself Elsie. When I woke up this morning I felt that bad I thought I HAD died!"

*Above: One of David Caswell's regular articles which appeared in The Vale Magazine in 2002.*

*Below: The children of Badsey First School sent David Caswell a card to celebrate the centenary of the family business in 2009.*

But, who knows, there may yet be someone out there happy to take on the role. Whilst the number of blacksmiths in the country is greatly reduced from a century or two ago, the blacksmith's trade is still alive in the Britain of the 21st century. A search of the internet reveals that there are courses on offer at places such as Warwickshire College, or there are a number of short traditional blacksmithing courses, for those seeking a change in their life. Perhaps in years to come we may still have a blacksmith working in Badsey.

In the meantime, congratulations to David Caswell on the 100th anniversary of his family business and a thank you to all blacksmiths past and present for the role they have played in our community.

## Notes

Information was drawn from the Badsey baptism, marriage and burial registers and the census returns, 1841-1901.

1 A bundle of 14 documents relating to the blacksmith's cottage and forge, rescued in the 1980s from being placed in a skip by Evesham solicitor, Peter Tucker, and donated to The Badsey Society by his widow, Anna.

2 Will of Henry Bird, Worcestershire Record Office, dated 29th June 1772, proved at Worcester, 5th February 1774.

3 Will of Samuel Oldaker, Worcestershire Record Office, dated 9th April 1839, proved at Worcester, 5th October 1839.

4 Conveyance of 1842 by William George Wilson to James Ashwin, Worcestershire Record Office, BA 7775, Ref 705:273 Parcel 36, Section (i).

5 *The Evesham Journal*, 1st February 1873.

6 Sales Particulars, 6th July 1891, Worcestershire Record Office, BA 7775, Ref 705:273 Parcel 28.

7 Deeds of Greystones, 10A High Street, in the possession of the current owners.

8 Aldington Enclosure Map, Worcestershire Record Office.

9 Arthur Savory, *Grain and Chaff from an English Manor*, 1920.

10 Parish Magazine, June 1962.

## Acknowledgments

With thanks to the following people: Anna Tucker, without whose kind donation of documents relating to the blacksmith's forge, demolished in the 1940s, this chapter would never have seen the light of day; Fred Roberts, a former occupier of the old blacksmith's cottage on Chapel Street; Stephen Entwistle and Gaynor Heath, the current owners of the building which was the forge in the late 19th century; Mick Thomas, the grandson of Frank Wheeler; and lastly, not forgetting the current blacksmith, David Caswell.

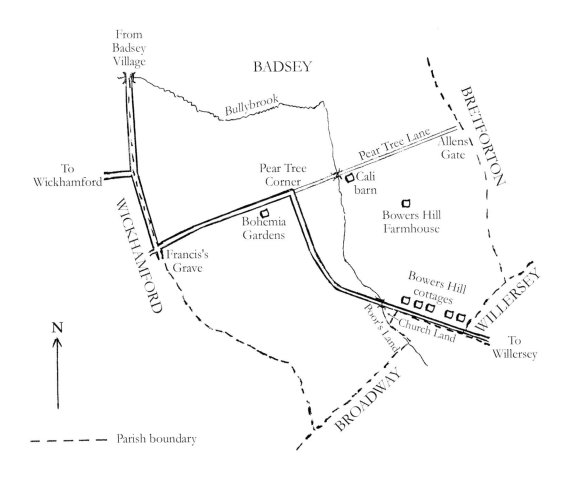

From
Badsey
Village

BADSEY

BRETFORTON

Bullybrook

Pear Tree Lane

Allens
Gate

To
Wickhamford

Pear Tree
Corner

Cali
barn

WICKHAMFORD

Bohemia
Gardens

Bowers Hill
Farmhouse

Francis's
Grave

Bowers Hill
cottages

WILLERSEY

N

Poor's Land

Church Land

To
Willersey

BROADWAY

– – – – Parish boundary

*A sketch map of the Bowers Hill area (not to scale).*

*Bowers Hill Farm today.*

# 2

# BOWERS HILL

## TERRY SPARROW

### Origin and Location

The part of Badsey known as Bowers Hill lies at the southern extremity of the parish, well away from the village centre. Perhaps because of its remoteness and sparse population it has so far not attracted much attention from local history writers, but this does not mean that the area has little of interest to reveal. But firstly, what is the origin of the name? Possibly the 'Hill' part is understandable, because whilst there is not any significant hill there, it is certainly higher than other parts of the parish. The 50 metre contour line passes very close to the Bowers Hill farmhouse, compared to, say, the centre of the village, where the height at the benchmark on the foot of the church tower is 123.1 feet, or 37.5 metres, above sea level. Turning now to the 'Bower' part of the name, this is more obscure. A search of the Badsey parish registers discloses no one named Bower or Bowers and the ordinary meaning of the word bower – an arbour or secluded place – does not seem to be particularly relevant. However, an alternative, virtually obsolete, definition may be worthy of our consideration. Here we see that a bower is (or was) a peasant or husbandman. Is this a clue? Is it too much to speculate that the name Bowers Hill originated as the place where a now long-forgotten labourer tilled the soil upon the little hill? Another theory, which possibly adds to the uncertainty, arises from examination of an indenture of 1824 regarding a lease of land occupied by Joseph Jones on both sides of Pear Tree Lane.[1] Among the field names listed in the document are Hither Buer's Hill and Far Buer's Hill. Is Buer's a corruption of Bowers, or vice versa? Probably we shall never know the answers.

It is difficult to say how far Bowers Hill extends. The limits of the farm itself are of course precise and easily identified, but how much of the surrounding area is included in the general description Bowers Hill? Northwards, in particular, the position is far from clear. For Parish Council representation Bowers Hill is a separate ward of Badsey parish and for that purpose embraces all properties as far north as the Bullybrook bridge. However, few people leaving the village along Willersey Road would consider themselves to be in Bowers Hill as soon as they crossed the brook. To take a broad, and perhaps arbitrary, view for the purpose of this chapter it will be assumed that Bowers Hill is that part of the parish of Badsey within half a mile or so of the farm.

## Roman Occupation

Largely due to the diligence of Arthur Edward Jones (1863-1950), a Badsey market gardener, several sites which indicate Roman occupation of the parish have been located. One of these sites is at Bowers Hill, in a field known as Black Ground, not far from the present day farmhouse. Here, coins of a number of Roman emperors were found, as well as other items of everyday use, including Samian pottery, whetstones (used for sharpening tools or weapons) and querns (hand mills for grinding corn).[2] Bearing in mind that the Roman road Icknield (or Ryknild) Street, also known locally as Buckle Street, passed within three miles of Bowers Hill, the discovery of these artefacts is hardly surprising. Nevertheless, there is insufficient evidence to suggest that any permanent settlement became established in the area. After the Roman legions left Britain we know nothing of any further habitation at Bowers Hill until the 19th century. When the Coventry surveyor Edward Phillips came to Badsey in 1812 at the time of the Enclosure Act and produced what is the earliest known detailed map of the whole parish, he recorded no dwellings whatsoever at Bowers Hill.

## The Enclosure Act of 1812

The Badsey Enclosure Act or, to quote its full title, *An Act for Inclosing Lands in the Parish of Badsey in the County of Worcester*, received the Royal Assent on 5th May 1812. Much has been written elsewhere concerning the enclosure, or fencing, of common land during the eighteenth and nineteenth centuries,

and a full review of the reasons behind enclosures, their benefits and their disadvantages, is outside the scope of this chapter. Suffice it to say that in 1812 the majority of the area we now know as Bowers Hill lay within the common fields of Badsey. Nevertheless, some 42 acres of the land there, in 13 separate plots, was already fenced in. These old enclosures, as they were described, belonged to the six persons named below, with their respective acreages also shown.

| | No. of separate plots | Total Area | | |
| --- | --- | --- | --- | --- |
| | | Acres | Roods | Perches |
| Thomas Byrd | 4 | 16 | 2 | 7 |
| Joseph Jones | 1 | 5 | 0 | 27 |
| John Procter | 3 | 10 | 0 | 26 |
| Edward Savage | 2 | 3 | 0 | 34 |
| Rev Thomas Williams | 1 | 3 | 0 | 18 |
| William Wilson | 2 | 3 | 3 | 9 |
| | 13 | 42 | 0 | 1 |

But the situation was soon to change. Once the Badsey Enclosure Act was in place the commissioners appointed to bring its provisions into effect, Frederick Phelps of Evesham and Henry Clarke of Shipston-upon-Stour, began their task of allotting the common land to those persons who were judged to be entitled to a share of it. The total area of such land within the parish was 851 acres 1 rood and 34 perches. (A rood is a quarter of an acre; a perch is one fortieth part of a rood). The commissioners were required, under the terms of the Act, to perform their duties '… according to equity and good conscience and without favour or affection, prejudice or partiality to any person or persons whomsoever'.

Phelps and Clarke finally published their awards on 1st July 1815. Following their allotments and various exchanges between the allottees the main three landowners in the Bowers Hill area, none of whom actually lived in Badsey, were the Dean and Chapter of Christ Church in Oxford, patrons of the ecclesiastical benefice of Badsey since 1546, the Reverend Charles Phillott, perpetual curate[3] of the benefice, and John Slatter of Salford Priors. Slatter (1790-1852) seems to have done quite well as a result of the Enclosure Act. Prior to that he was already a Badsey landowner, with four old enclosures in the Claybrook area plus sundry pieces in the common fields, but following the implementation of the Act the whole of his Badsey estate, amounting to 86 acres, was conveniently located in one holding. This was to become Bowers Hill Farm and, soon afterwards, a house and farm buildings were erected there in a field known as Peartree Close. Its present day National Grid reference is SP 086420.

## Bowers Hill Farm

On 25th March 1818 John Slatter sold the farm to William Collett. It is clear that a complete farmstead had been created during the period 1815-1818, as the sale contract refers to '... all that new erected messuage, cottage or tenement with barn, stables and other outbuildings ... now in occupation of Thomas Smith'.[4] Collett lived in Badsey village centre at the house now known as The Firs and it is unlikely that he ever occupied Bowers Hill himself. Certainly by 1833, and possibly earlier, William Henry Smith was there as tenant farmer. It is not known whether there was any family connection between Thomas and William Smith. The Badsey Poor Rate Assessment made on 12th June 1833 lists William Smith as occupier of Collett's property, which had a rateable value of £100, with the rate being levied at sixpence in the pound.[5] William Collett died in 1850 and his wife Mary in 1865, following which the ownership of Bowers Hill Farm passed in equal shares to her nephews Thomas Yardington Tovey and William Tovey[6], who already farmed considerable acreages in their home village of Church Lench. According to Mary Collett's will dated 9th October 1863, William Smith was still the tenant farmer at Bowers Hill, although the 1861 census indicates that he was then no longer living there. Among other legacies Mary left £10 to the Badsey churchwardens, to be used for the purchase of blankets to be given to poor villagers at Christmas following her death.

In 1866 William Tovey, finding himself in need of funds and using his share of the inherited property as security, borrowed £600 from Herbert New, gentleman, of Evesham[7] who, in truth, was mortgagee in name only, as trustee for Charles Harries Jones who actually found the money. By then William Smith's long tenancy had come to an end and a new man, John Rimell, had arrived. But he did not stay for long and as the 19th century progressed towards its conclusion Bowers Hill Farm saw frequent changes of occupier, probably due to the precarious state of the farming industry at the time. In 1871 Frederick Luxton was the tenant farmer; in 1891 it was William Foden; in 1894 James Mapstone and, as a new century dawned, Francis Hoddinott. The precise dates of these tenancies are obscure and possibly there were others. We do know that for a period, between the departure of Luxton and the arrival of Foden, the Tovey family farmed Bowers Hill themselves. Certainly Thomas Yardington Tovey occupied the farm in 1879 when, like his younger brother before him, he approached Herbert New for a loan. Again the security was a half share of Bowers Hill Farm, although this time New funded the mortgage himself. It was for £500. When the census of population was taken in 1881 Elizabeth Tovey, widow of William, who had died in 1875, was living at Bowers Hill and is described as a farmer of 99 acres. Her eldest son, also William, was the farm manager.

In 1892 Herbert New transferred Thomas Tovey's mortgage to E G Righton of Evesham and J B Workman of Hampton[7]. New died on 28th November 1893 and the following September his executors assigned the earlier mortgage to Charles Harries Jones[7]. Jones died a few days later and on 9th September 1895 his executors joined with Righton and Workman to offer the whole of Bowers Hill Farm for sale by public auction at the Kings Head Hotel in Evesham. Thus they exercised their right under the terms of the mortgages to sell the property if there were arrears of principal or interest. The purchaser was Henry Byrd of 83 High Street, Evesham; the purchase price was £1410.[7]

As from Lady Day 1898 Byrd let the farm to John Idiens on a 21 year lease at a rent of £130 per annum[7] but it is not clear to what extent, if at all, Idiens actually farmed the land himself. Presumably Francis Hoddinott, who certainly was there in 1901 – he later moved to Aston Magna – was merely a sub tenant. One interesting condition of the lease was the obligation for Idiens to plant certain fields, about 35 acres in total, with fruit trees, the work to be carried out by 1st March 1899. John Idiens was living in Evesham at the time when the lease was granted, but shortly afterwards the family moved to Wickhamford Manor, where the 1901 census recorded John as a coal merchant. From 1902 to

1904 he served as a manager of Badsey School. In the event his Bowers Hill lease did not run its full course and following Henry Byrd's death in 1904 Byrd's nephew and five nieces, who inherited the farm, sold it on 13th April 1905 for £3000 to John Idiens and Sons Limited, an incorporated company whose registered office was at 91 High Street, Evesham[7]. John Idiens was one of the directors of that company.

Possibly mindful that Badsey's emergent market garden industry, leading to a growing population, was creating a demand for more housing in the parish, the company decided to build fourteen semidetached cottages at the farm, fronting the Willersey Road. On 18th May 1905 they borrowed £7000 in order to finance the scheme. The lender was W B Cregoe-Colmore, who did not manage his own affairs for health reasons, so that the mortgage was actually in the names of his trustees J C O'Neal and W J Halsey. The application was for a total of £8000, with £500 to be deferred until seven of the cottages had been built and the remaining £500 held over until completion of the project.[7] In the event, only ten were built and it seems doubtful whether any money beyond the original £7000 was ever advanced. On 18th October 1905 John Idiens and Sons Limited entered into a contract with the General Land Drainage and Improvement Company to install a water supply to the new cottages, at a cost of £2285 3s 0d, payable over 40 years at £55 7s 7d every half year. This appears to have been some kind of government-backed arrangement, as the schedule of repayments, divided between capital and interest, appears in *An Absolute Order of the Board of Agriculture and Fisheries, no. 1133a,* dated 16th November 1907.[7] The security mentioned in this order was not only Bowers Hill Farm, but also '... a portion of The Stockey in Badsey owned by the United Counties Bank Limited'. The Bowers Hill occupier at the time was said to be Harold Idiens and The Avon Orchard Company.

The reference to the Stockey arises because Idiens Limited, supported by funding from the United Counties Bank Limited, was undertaking other building work in Badsey, on part of the Stockey field, comprising the erection of a terrace of fourteen houses and a smithy. These houses were known as numbers 1 to 14 Stockey Piece Cottages,

Bullybrook Road. Later, the address became 1 to 14 Cotswold View; today it is even numbers 34 to 60 Willersey Road. Here, too, a contract with the General Land Drainage and Improvement Company was in place – *An Absolute Order of the Board of Agriculture and Fisheries, no. 1133,* refers – and it appears that both loans were secured against both the Bowers Hill and Stockey properties. This situation continued until August 1911, when two Deeds of Release separated the securities.[7]

It is difficult to imagine how the Idiens' building venture at Bowers Hill could ever have been viable. Interest alone on the original mortgage was £280 per annum (assuming no capital repayments) and it is unlikely that the ten cottages would have yielded rents of more than £13 per annum each. It is hardly surprising that the company very quickly found itself in serious financial trouble. On 22nd August 1911 W J Halsey and his co-trustee A A Barnard, who had replaced O'Neal deceased, paid off the drainage company's loan; then, three months later, they commenced an action against Idiens Limited in the Chancery Division of the High Court of Justice (No. H2865 of 1911). The company was given time to pay but did not do so and on 17th September 1912 the Court made an order "... in an action in which W J Halsey and A A Barnard were plaintiffs and John Idiens and Sons Limited and the United Counties Bank Limited were defendants, whereby the defendants were foreclosed from all rights ... of the Bowers Hill Estate". Thus Idiens' interest in Bowers Hill Farm came to a sad but inevitable end. Four years later John Idiens and Sons Limited was dissolved and its name struck off the register.[8]

Meanwhile, another tenant had come and gone. James de Radcliffe Openshaw arrived at Bowers Hill, probably in 1906 or 1907; telephone directories list him as a florist and fruit grower, whilst the 1911 edition of *Smith's Household Almanack* describes him as a tomato and fruit grower. It seems that he erected several greenhouses near the Willersey road and when he left the premises in June 1911 a dispute arose regarding compensation due to him. E G Righton was appointed as arbitrator under the provisions of the Agricultural Holdings Act 1908 and he awarded Openshaw £1200 9s 11d, which included £928 for six greenhouses with fittings and a packing shed and £241 for growing crops. On the other hand, £492 1s 3d was deducted from the amount due to him, mainly to cover arrears of rent.[7] The next tenant was Bernard Barton, listed in *Kelly's Directory* for 1916 as a fruit grower. More about him will be written later in the chapter. Mention of both Openshaw and Barton as fruit growers does tend to confirm that the obligation to plant fruit trees at the farm, as a condition of the 1898 lease, had been properly fulfilled. About 1918 another tenant, Albert Ernest Gray, arrived but, like many of his predecessors, he stayed for only a few years.

W B Cregoe-Colmore died on 18th December 1918. A certificate issued by the Inland Revenue in 1923 to confirm that the relevant Estate Duty had been paid lists his Bowers Hill property as follows:

1  Bowers Hill Farm
2  Allotment land fronting Willersey and Badsey road
3  8 glasshouses and other buildings
4  10 cottages fronting said road

The first valuation of this property was £11000, finally reduced to £10190. It appears that difficulties arose in winding up the estate – the Public Trustee became involved following A A Barnard's death in June 1919 – and it was not until June 1920 that Cregoe-Colmore's will was proved. On 23rd January 1924 Bowers Hill Farm, with just one of the cottages (no. 10) was sold to Johnson Thornely of Chester for £4635. His younger brother Frederick went there as tenant farmer. Frederick Thornely had farmed in Canada for some years before the 1914-1918 War; during the war he served in France as an officer in the Canadian Engineers and was wounded in action. Unfortunately his business at Bowers Hill was not particularly successful. A bank overdraft facility for £500 guaranteed by his brother Johnson had almost reached its limit and he became severely depressed regarding his financial situation. On 24th December 1928 Captain Thornely went to the edge of a well on a neighbour's land and shot himself in the head. Police recovered his body from the well the following day, together with the shotgun. The coroner, on hearing that there appeared to be no suspicious circumstances, returned a verdict of 'suicide while temporarily insane'.[9]

Soon after the tragic death of Frederick Thornely his sister Margaret and her husband Buckley Bent, who were living at The Parks, Aldington, moved to Bowers Hill, but ownership of the property remained with Johnson Thornely until his death in 1947. In due course his personal representatives sold the farm to Ralph Thornely Bent (son of Buckley) for £5600. Six months later, on 18th September 1951, Ralph, who lived and worked in Peru, sold Bowers Hill Farm, which still included no. 10 Bowers Hill Cottages, at the same price, to his brother John Martin Bent, who was already there as tenant. John Bent died in 1985 and the following year his widow Evelyn sold no. 10 to J H Wayland. Since that time there have been several family arrangements; some land has been sold and in 2006 the old farm buildings were tastefully converted into residential accommodation. Bowers Hill Farm is still a small working mixed farm but, in addition, the present owner, John's elder son Martin Buckley Bent, together with his wife Sarah, run a guest house at their home.

## The Poor's Land

Having a frontage of about 100 yards to the Willersey road and extending in a southerly direction to reach the parish boundary between Badsey and Broadway, lies the Poor's Land. It is a pasture field, about 9 acres (3.65 hectares) in area and it is the permanent endowment of the Aldington and Badsey Relief in Need Charity. This charity, albeit in a different form, was set up more than 300 years ago by the public-spirited action of five Badsey and Aldington parishioners. Their names are recorded on the charity board in St James Church, as shown below:

> Mr Thomas Martin of Aldington gave five Pounds
> Mrs Jane Jarret of ye same gave 5 Pounds
> Mr Aug'tn Jarret of ye same gave 20 Pounds
> Mrs Eliz: George of Badsey gave 7 Pounds
> Mr Jar't Stephens of ye same gave 6 Pounds

We are also told '… the above sums were given to the Poor, that they might have the use thereof for ever in Bread'.

Unfortunately the board is not dated and to get some idea of when the money was given we must rely on other sources of information, in particular the ornate marble tablet, fixed to the north wall of the church, in memory of the Jarrett family. Here we can see that Jane Jarrett (the spelling of the name on the monument differs slightly from that on the

*Preamble to the Scheme for regulation of the Aldington and
Badsey Charities from 5th May 1978.*

charity board) died in 1683, two years after the death
of her husband, and it is more than likely that she
established her part of the charity during her
widowhood. Her son Augustin may well have
donated his £20 around the same time; he did not
survive his mother for long and his burial is recorded
in the Badsey register on 2nd December 1685. Also
in the register we find the baptisms of two persons
named Thomas Martin, in 1610 and 1639
respectively. Neither appears to have been buried
at Badsey; probably one of them was the benefactor
named on the charity board. As for Elizabeth
George, the position is even more uncertain. A
monument in Badsey churchyard, still clearly legible,
marks the grave of Elizabeth, the wife of Robert

George, who 'dyed Febr. the 26th 1644'.
Furthermore, the register confirms the burials of
two other persons named Elizabeth George, in 1712
and 1714 respectively, the latter being the last
mention of a George in Badsey. And finally, Jarrett
Stephens, who was buried here in 1732, the last
Stephens to be mentioned in parish records. All of
this suggests the origin of these charities to be
between the mid-seventeenth and early eighteenth
centuries; it is most unlikely that all were set up at
the same time.

The money provided by the five benefactors,
£43 in total, was used to purchase sundry pieces of
land lying dispersed in the common fields of the
parish, with the intention that income generated
from letting should be used to provide bread for
needy parishioners. We know that in 1694 £2 7s 8d
was received from Charles Welch for 'ye Poor's
Land' and that £1 10s 0d was paid to 'ye baker' for
bread at Easter and Christmas[10]. Following the
Enclosure Act of 1812 the dispersed pieces were
consolidated into a single holding although, strictly,
there were two separate awards by the
commissioners; the first "... unto the
Churchwardens and Overseers of the Poor of the
Parish of Badsey ... in lieu of and for their right of
cutting furze and bushes growing in and upon Dry
Leys and Old Leys ... land situate in Meerden Field
containing two roods and thirty-eight perches", and
the second "... unto the Churchwardens and
Overseers of the Poor of the Parish of Badsey and
the Hamlet of Aldington ... in lieu of the
Commonable part of their estate and right of
Common thereunto belonging ... land situate in
Meerden Field containing eight acres one rood and
twenty-one perches". These two adjoining pieces
of land were immediately merged and form the
present-day Poor's Land. The five charities remained
separate, but to all intents and purposes were
administered as one, usually known as the Bread
Charity.

One assumes that the churchwardens and
overseers did their best to ensure that the bread
was allocated in an equitable manner, but apparently
their choice of recipients did not always please
everyone. In November 1872 the Reverend Thomas
Hunt reported to Christ Church that the Bread
Charity was '... a cause of much ill will and strife'.
He expressed the opinion that it would be far better

if the charity was converted into aid towards mental food and used as an endowment for the school. But the distribution of free bread to the poor of Badsey and Aldington continued until 1978, at which point there were 17 beneficiaries each receiving two loaves a month. Then, the trustees having decided that it would be advantageous to alter the terms of the charity, a new scheme was approved by the Charity Commissioners on 5th May 1978. The five former charities were amalgamated into one under the title 'Aldington and Badsey Relief in Need Charity'. Within its terms the trustees are authorised to assist persons resident in Aldington and Badsey who are "... in conditions of need, hardship or distress, by making grants of money or paying for items, services or facilities calculated to reduce the need, hardship or distress of such persons".

## The Church Land

The Church Land, a small meadow of about $1\frac{1}{2}$ acres, is situated in the angle between the Willersey road and the Poor's Land and is separated from the latter by the brook. For almost five centuries, possibly longer, Badsey Church owned land within the common fields of the parish, although its precise location is unknown. It seems that for a time the churchwardens were responsible for working the land, with the resulting crop of corn being sold for the benefit of church funds. This may be illustrated by an entry in the wardens' accounts for 1530-31: 'reseuyd of ye gedrynge of ye corne xxxiii d' (received of the gathering of the corn 33 pence). Similar entries occur in subsequent years. Sometimes there was expenditure relating to the land, as in 1544-45: 'payyd for ye eryge of ye churche acur vi d' (paid for ploughing the church acre 6 pence). Later, the land was let; entries during the seventeenth and eighteenth centuries indicate a rental income of 7 shillings per annum.[11] Then came the Enclosure Act, and Badsey Church was granted a fenced meadow in lieu of the former holding in the common fields. The commissioners awarded "Unto the Churchwardens of the Parish of Badsey and their successors in lieu of the commonable part of their estate and right of common thereto belonging, all that allotment or parcel of land situate in Foxhill Field containing one acre and one rood and thirty-four perches ...".

But the Foxhill land was immediately exchanged "... and the said commissioners hereby assign allot and award in exchange to the said Thomas Byrd and his heirs, all that the aforesaid allotment or parcel of land containing one acre one rood and thirty-four perches being the allotment herein awarded to the Churchwardens of Badsey ... in lieu of and in exchange for all that piece of inclosed land herein before described." The award goes on to say "... and the said commissioners hereby assign allot and award in exchange unto the said Churchwardens and their successors, all that the said piece or parcel of inclosed land called Condercope Meadow containing one acre two roods and nine perches in lieu of and in exchange for the said allotment so awarded to the said Churchwardens as aforesaid". The outcome of this exchange was that the wardens finished up with a slightly larger piece of land, but almost certainly one of inferior quality. The rent from letting Condercope Meadow is applied for general church maintenance. In 1872 the Reverend Thomas Hunt reported that the rent was £3 per year. Later it was reduced, to £2 in 1881 and to £1 10s 0d in 1898, presumably because of the depressed state of the farming industry. At the present time the annual rent is £78.

## Pear Tree Lane

In 1815 the Enclosure Commissioners listed a mere nine roads in Badsey, although they were of four distinct kinds. These were:

a public turnpike road (of which there was only one);

b public carriage road and highway (three);

c private carriage road and drift way[12] (four);

d public bridle road and private carriage road and drift way (one).

The latter, named on the Enclosure Map as Pear Tree Lane, is the track from Pear Tree Corner and is described as "... of the breadth of twenty feet marked no. 5 commencing at the Willersey Road and extending in an eastwardly direction until it communicates with the parish of Bretforton at Allens Gate, the carriage road for the use of the proprietors of the land adjoining". Thus it was a public thoroughfare for travellers on foot or horseback, whereas any other access, for example by carts or herds of animals, was restricted to

*Pear Tree Corner. A view looking north painted by Ian Gibson.*

owners and occupiers of the land on either side of the road.

This road, never of much importance to the majority of Badsey's population, became the subject of disputes regarding responsibility for its repair and maintenance, although the Enclosure Award seems to be quite clear in the matter, directing that "... the private carriage roads shall be made and repaired at the expense of the parties required by law to repair the public roads in the parish", in other words the ratepayers. In 1838 Joseph Jones (1771-1853), the Badsey road surveyor at the time, gravelled Pear Tree Lane and charged the cost to public funds, which appears to have been the correct procedure. But the parish protested to the magistrates who, possibly mindful that Jones was tenant of most of the land adjoining the road and therefore its most regular user, ordered him to refund the money. It is not known whether he was able to obtain a contribution from the landowner, the Dean and Chapter of Christ Church.

Then, in 1875, the Evesham District Highway Board, which by then had control of the parish roads, ordered Badsey ratepayers to repair Pear Tree Lane. This order led to strong protests from the Badsey people. Vestry meetings were called; resolutions were passed; lengthy correspondence ensued between Reverend Hunt, the Highway Board and the land agent for the Dean and Chapter; it is a splendid example of 19th century parish politics.[5] The final outcome is not known, although the available correspondence between the parties does suggest that a compromise may have been reached.

Just off Pear Tree Lane, about 250 yards from Pear Tree Corner, lies the substantial brick-built barn known to local people as Cali Barn, although the precise spelling is uncertain. No one seems to know whether it is Cali or Cally or Calais; however, one former occupier of the barn, who in 1975 erected a high fence around it and named it *Fort Calais*, clearly believed that the latter version is the correct one. No building at this location is indicated on Edward Phillips's 1812 map, whereas one is shown on the Ordnance Survey Map of 1828, suggesting that the barn was erected about the same time as the house at Bowers Hill Farm, although any specific connection between them is unlikely. At least one modern map[13] describes the building as a Tithe Barn, but it is difficult to accept that it was ever used as such, given that the Badsey tithes were extinguished by the Enclosure Act, thus removing the need for a tithe barn. An area of land near the barn is also known as Cali (or Cally or Calais) and it seems likely that the barn was named after the land rather than vice versa. The present writer recalls a story told to him many years ago which, if true, does explain the origin of the name. It relates to a 19th century market gardener who acquired the tenancy of some of the land and, hoping to make his fortune from the new venture and knowing of the Californian gold rush of 1849, nicknamed his land California, soon abbreviated to Cali.

### Francis's Grave

About half a mile beyond the Bullybrook bridge the Willersey Road turns sharply eastwards. This corner, a little way before we reach Bowers Hill as defined in the first section of this chapter, has for many years been known as Francis's Grave, although the reason why it is thus known is uncertain. A document of 1781 tells us that Edward Cooper "... hath contracted to buy ... all those sellions or rudges[14] or pieces or parcels of arable, meadow and pasture ... lying dispersed in the open and common fields and commonable places of Badsey".[15] Included in the purchase was "... In Meerden Field, one rudge of land in Francis's Grave Furlong". It seems reasonable to assume that this refers to the furlong either containing, or adjacent to, Francis's Grave. (A furlong, in this case, is an area 220 yards long and 22 yards wide, equal to one acre). In 1815 the Enclosure Commissioners described the Willersey Road as "... leading in a southwardly direction to Frances Grave". (Notice the slightly different spelling). But who was Francis, or Frances? Was it the person's Christian name or surname? Why was he, or she, buried at this spot?

The Reverend Peter Braby, vicar of Badsey with Aldington and also of Wickhamford from 1958 to 1973, who was a keen student of local history, thought that it might be the burial place of a suicide or murderer.[16] Presumably such a person would have been denied burial in the churchyard and, instead, interred well away from the village centre. Given that the land immediately to the west of the corner lies in the parish of Wickhamford, the grave could just as easily be in that parish as in Badsey. Some

credence was given to Rev Braby's theory when he discovered a particular entry, which the present writer has also seen, in the Wickhamford Manor Court papers. There we can read that on 22nd October 1639, at the Court of Samuel Sandys (Lord of the Manor of Wickhamford) a man named Thomas Francis was presented for homicide and, as a result, his lands and goods were forfeited to the lord.[17]

On 19th September 1927 workmen engaged in laying a culvert and widening the road at the corner unearthed a human skeleton. Local antiquarian Arthur Jones was soon summoned to the scene and concluded that the skeleton was that of a woman; he thought it was between 200 and 300 years old. *The Evesham Journal*, in its report of the incident, said that it was a custom to bury suicides at a crossroads, which this location is, if the still existing farm tracks are taken into account. But this was merely a generalisation; no firm evidence was produced to support a case of suicide. Possibly the woman's name was Frances; almost certainly we shall never know. Then, on 13th October, the same workmen found a second skeleton, just a few yards from the first. Again Jones was consulted; this time he formed the opinion that it was a male adult, possibly 1500 years old. The District Coroner reached an open verdict at the subsequent inquest, ruling that the bones were probably several hundred years old.[18] So there were graves at this lonely spot; of that there can be no doubt and perhaps there are more discoveries to come. But the true identity of Francis, or Frances, remains a mystery.

### A Case of Manslaughter

One of the shortest tenancies at Bowers Hill Farm, and one which ended in tragedy, was that of James Mapstone, originally from Somerset, who came to Badsey with his wife and three children in 1894. The two elder children were enrolled at Badsey School in April of that year. It seems that Mapstone was soon faced with financial problems and on 14th March 1895, with £7 10s still owing on a loan, the moneylenders sent bailiffs to take possession of goods in settlement of the debt. The farmer was ploughing when they arrived. One of the bailiffs, William Dawson, said that he would have possession of the horses and a struggle followed, during which Dawson struck Mapstone with a heavy stick, knocking him to the ground and leaving him with a severe head wound and a badly lacerated finger. On 25th March James Mapstone died from acute tetanus which, according to medical evidence given at the inquest into the death, was a result of the injury to the finger. Dawson denied striking Mapstone at all and said the injury was caused by the deceased getting his hand entangled in the harness of a horse he was holding. However, the inquest jury, after hearing several witnesses, returned a verdict of manslaughter, whereupon Dawson was committed on the coroner's warrant for trial at Worcester Assizes.

On 26th June 1895, at the Summer Assizes at the Shirehall in Worcester, William Dawson was indicted for 'feloniously killing and slaying' James Mapstone at Badsey on 14th March. There was also a second indictment for manslaughter on the coroner's warrant. Dawson pleaded not guilty but, rather strangely, his colleague Evans was not called as a witness for the defence. The Court heard evidence from a number of prosecution witnesses, after which the defending solicitor addressed the jury at length, saying that it was not a case where such an amount of violence had been used that it was almost certain that death must result. Mr Justice Hawkins, in summing up, said there was no evidence to justify the violence, which therefore might be taken as unlawful, and if by an unlawful act of violence the death of another was caused, then the person causing that death was guilty of manslaughter. The jury, without leaving the box, returned a verdict of guilty. Sentence was deferred that day. On his return to the court, the judge said that Dawson let his temper get the better of what ought to have been his judgement. A sentence of eight months in prison, with hard labour, was imposed.[19]

James Mapstone was buried in Badsey churchyard on 30th March 1895. His widow Sarah, who left Badsey soon after his death, was buried with him on 3rd February 1933; the burial register gives her address as Chew Stoke, a village in Somerset. When the Badsey church bells were dismantled, repaired and re-hung in 1950, the board which records the event shows that one of the bells was restored as a memorial to James and Sarah Mapstone. It is perhaps surprising that a couple who lived in Badsey for less than two years, more than half a century before the bells were restored, should be remembered in this way.

## Lieutenant Colonel Bernard Barton

Bernard Barton, who was born in 1879 at Fridaythorpe in Yorkshire, where his father was the vicar, came to Bowers Hill Farm shortly before the First World War. He had seen service in the Boer War of 1899-1902. In August 1914 he enlisted in the local company of Territorials and later that year was commissioned in the Worcestershire Regiment. On 21st September 1915, following promotion to captain, he went to France with the newly formed 11th battalion of the regiment and it is unlikely that he ever returned to Bowers Hill. Later, Captain Barton was posted to Salonika, where he was mentioned in despatches, promoted to major and then severely wounded, necessitating his return to England in the spring of 1917. About a year later he went back to France and on 20th June 1918 was appointed as commanding officer of the 2nd/8th battalion Worcestershire Regiment, with the rank of lieutenant colonel. On 11th August the battalion was in a forward position near the village of Merville, on the bank of the River Lys, and there Bernard Barton was killed by an enemy bomb.[20] He is buried at Tannay British Cemetery at Thiennes in France and he is commemorated on the war memorial in Badsey Church.

Although Barton had a distinguished military career his short-lived business venture at Bowers Hill ended rather sadly. In June 1916 Cregoe-Colmore's trustees, W J Halsey and A A Barnard, applied to the Court at Evesham for possession of the farm, stating that the tenant, Barton, had deserted it, leaving it uncultivated and unoccupied and with £290 arrears of rent. The justices of the peace, James Ashwin of Bretforton and C A Binyon of Badsey, after visiting the farm, granted possession. A similar application, with a similar outcome, was made to the Chipping Campden justices in respect of a small part of the farm which lay in the parish of Willersey.[7]

Another Bowers Hill resident named on Badsey's war memorial is Lance-corporal Henry S Hancock. He was born about 1898 at Cow Honeybourne, the second of five children of Richard and Mary Emma Hancock, and it seems likely that the family came to live at No 1 Bowers Hill Cottages in 1914, as Henry's two younger brothers, Joseph and Leslie, were enrolled at Badsey School in November of that year. Henry Hancock was killed in action on 7th December 1917 whilst serving with the 7th battalion Kings Shropshire Light Infantry. He is buried in France at Favreuil British Cemetery. The Hancock family continued to live at 1 Bowers Hill until a few years ago.

## Bohemia Gardens

About 200 yards west of Pear Tree Corner a collection of dilapidated sheds marks the site of a bungalow, known as Bohemia Gardens, which was built in the early years of the 20th century. Its original owner was the strangely named Frederick Ingledew Hooper Ingledew. He was born at Worcester in 1857 and then named Frederick Ingledew Hooper (Ingledew was his mother's maiden name), spent some years in America, where he married, before returning to England. By 1901 the family had changed their surname to Ingledew and were living at Wickhamford, where Frederick was in business as a fruit grower. A few years later the Ingledews purchased land in Willersey Road and Bohemia Gardens was built there. The precise date is not known, but the National Telephone Company's directory for 1906-07 lists 'F I H Ingledew, Bohemia Gardens, telephone number Badsey 11'. In 1912 *Kelly's Directory* lists Frederick as a market gardener. From 1903 to 1906 he served as a manager of Badsey School. The Ingledews left Badsey about 1914 and it appears that the name 'Bohemia Gardens' went out of use after their departure. W & H Smith's Household Almanack from 1915 onwards gives the address of subsequent occupiers, first H Powell and then Major Hugh Ingram, as simply 'The Bungalow, Bowers Hill'.

Late one Saturday evening in 1934, while Ingram and his wife were away from home, the bungalow caught fire. The alarm was raised by another Willersey Road resident, Charles Seabright, and the fire brigade was summoned. When the brigade arrived they were unable to connect to the nearest adequate water supply because their hose was of insufficient length and while they were fetching more hose from their station '... the bungalow had become a raging mass of flame and the glow in the midnight moonless sky was visible for miles around'.[21] Although some furniture and other contents were salvaged the building was a total loss. Walls and chimneys which were left standing after the fire gradually collapsed with the passage of time so that little sign of a bungalow now remains.

## Allotments and Market Gardens

During the latter part of the 19th century, when British agriculture was experiencing a long period of depression, almost all of Badsey's farmland was split up into small market garden holdings. It was a gradual process, at first quite slow, but then gaining momentum after about 1880. This may be illustrated by looking at the numbers of Badsey people engaged in market gardening, as recorded in the censuses.

| | |
|---|---|
| 1871 | 21 |
| 1881 | 44 |
| 1891 | 120 |
| 1901 | 196 |

The figures include those who are variously described as market gardener, market gardener's son (of working age), market gardener's labourer, gardener or gardener's labourer. The total population of Badsey – men, women and children – in 1901 was 775. It is not known precisely when market gardening became established in the Bowers Hill area, nor which fields were first used for that purpose. We do, however, know that Bowers Hill Farm itself remained as a complete unit throughout this time of change although, as pointed out earlier, there was a partial shift from conventional farming to fruit growing as the new century dawned.

Some farmland – about 54 acres – to the north of Pear Tree Lane was divided into allotments as shown in the illustration. Unfortunately, neither the plan nor its accompanying schedule of tenants' names is dated, but an examination of other documents at the same source[22] suggests a date circa 1850. These allotments, whose location is easily recognised by reference to the Badsey Enclosure Map, were part of the land awarded in 1815 to the Dean and Chapter of Christ Church and which at that time was leased to John Millard, John Benton (both of Pebworth) and Ann Slatter, widow (mother of John Slatter, mentioned earlier as the owner of Bowers Hill Farm for a brief period until 1818). Subsequently there was a series of leases, usually renewed at seven year intervals, from Christ Church to various members of the Slatter family.

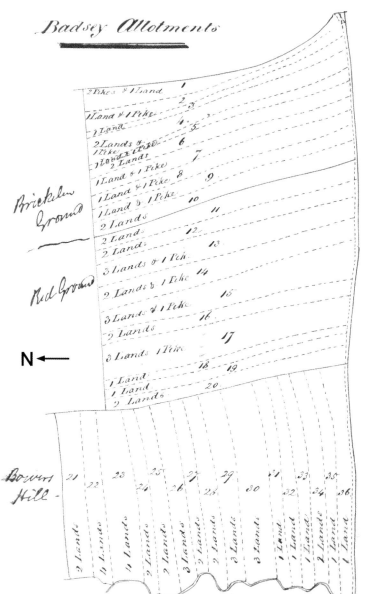

*Badsey Allotments*

provides reasonably conclusive evidence that the allotments on 54 acres of the land were created about the middle of the century. Subsequent lists of tenants, but without plans, indicate that most, if not all, of the Christ Church land was divided into allotments by the early 1860s.[22]

But what is an allotment? Does the division of fields in the Bowers Hill area tell us that market gardening was about to begin there as early as, say, the period 1850-1860? It would seem not, if we accept, as surely we must, that the census returns provide the most reliable source for determining the occupation of Badsey people. The conclusion must be that these small plots of land were not initially market gardens, but were merely used to grow crops – probably corn for bread making as well as vegetables – solely for home consumption by tenants whose main occupation lay elsewhere. For example, Thomas Hall, one of the early Christ Church allotment holders, was a cordwainer (shoemaker); others included William Allchurch, a stone cutter, and Richard Oldaker the blacksmith, but the majority were farm labourers.

Around the same time when the Christ Church allotments were becoming established a similar scene was unfolding on the Badsey glebe land, the bulk of which also lay in the Bowers Hill area. In

This situation continued until 10th October 1874, at which point the then lessees – the trustees of the marriage settlement of William Stubbs and his wife Hannah, formerly Slatter – surrendered the unexpired portion of the existing lease.[22] However, it is doubtful whether these respective lessees ever worked the land themselves. For many years they, in turn, leased it to a Badsey farmer, Joseph Jones and several indentures, the latest one in 1849, confirm his tenancy of almost 140 acres of Christ Church land. But Jones died in 1853 and this

1815 this land was awarded by the enclosure commissioners to the Reverend Charles Phillott. R W Sidwell[23] quotes from information supplied to him by the Reverend P Braby to the effect that about 1841 some of the glebe land was let out in small lots of about one or two acres each. Sidwell goes on to say that over the mid-century period the whole of the glebe land passed into market garden smallholdings. However, there appears to be no evidence to support the latter statement. The census of 1871 is the first for Badsey in which the term 'market gardener' appears and, furthermore, we know that in 1872 the Reverend Thomas Hunt was still farming part, at least, of the glebe himself.[16] We can only conclude that those first glebe allotments were, like the ones on the Christ Church land, simply a means of providing for the needs of the tenants and their families. It seems reasonable to assume that the growth of market gardening, whether on the Christ Church Estate, the Glebe Farm or anywhere else in the Bowers Hill area, mirrored the situation in the remainder of the parish and only reached a significant level during the last two decades of the 19th century. In recent years the scene has been reversed; market gardening has all but disappeared. Sheep now graze to the north of Pear Tree Lane and much of the nearby land again yields cereal crops.

## A Wartime Tragedy

A fatal aeroplane crash occurred at Bowers Hill on 31st August 1942. The aircraft involved in the tragedy was an Armstrong Whitworth Whitley Mark V bomber, based at the wartime Honeybourne aerodrome, home of no. 24 Operational Training Unit, Royal Air Force, which was less than two miles as the crow flies from Bowers Hill Farm. The Whitley had been engaged in local flying for training purposes and on return to the airfield the pilot unfortunately misjudged his approach, overshot the runway and hit a tree, causing part of one wing to fall off the plane. The crippled aircraft climbed slightly, the pilot probably intending to complete another circuit before making a second attempt to land on the runway. However, it remained airborne only as far as Bowers Hill, where it crashed and burst into flames. Of the three man crew only one survived; sadly, both pilots, Flight Sergeant W H Terwilliger and Sergeant G W West, were killed. The former was a member of the Royal Canadian Air Force; he is buried at Waterside Cemetery in Evesham.[24]

## The Cottages

The Bowers Hill cottages, built by John Idiens and Sons Limited about 1906, at first had many changes of occupier. Tenants such as William Langfield, market gardener, and Walter Jones, market gardener and coal merchant, moved in and out within the space of a few years. But once this initial coming and going was over a fairly settled community

developed, with several families living in the same houses for very long periods. Walter Cull, eldest son of John Cull the Badsey baker, moved into no. 6 with his wife and children during the first world war; later, other children were born there. The Cull family is still at Bowers Hill today. The Hancocks – more than 80 years at no. 1 – have already been mentioned, whilst the families of Bayliss, Chamberlain, Huxley, Jelfs and Phillips lived in one or other of the cottages for periods ranging from about 30 to 50 years. The Phillips family, who lived at no. 5, ran a nursery business at the nearby glasshouses. Among the current residents is Seymour Smith, who has been at no. 7 for 38 years.

It is not entirely clear when the ownership of the cottages changed hands during the years following the death of W B Cregoe-Colmore. It is fairly certain that all except no. 10 were purchased by Worcestershire County Council, but not necessarily at the same time. In 1924, an Abstract of Title of the Public Trustee and others as trustees of Cregoe-Colmore's will states '... for the purpose of raising money for legacies, funeral expenses, etc, certain parts of the Bowers Hill property have been sold from time to time'. Most of the cottages are now privately owned; only nos. 7 and 8 are retained by the County Council; these two were bought by the Council on 4th November 1926.

The barn conversion at the farm in 2006, which created five new residential units, was the largest building project in the Bowers Hill area since the ten cottages were erected a century earlier. Less than a dozen other dwellings have appeared there during the intervening years. Bowers Hill remains as a somewhat isolated part of Badsey parish and any significant development in the foreseeable future seems unlikely.

## Notes

(WRO = Worcestershire Record Office; EJ = *Evesham Journal and Four Shires Advertiser*).

1    Warwickshire County Record Office. CR1596/Box 81/2/13.
2    B G Cox : *Romano-British Occupation Sites in the Vale of Evesham* (Research Papers of the Vale of Evesham Historical Society, volume I, 1967).
3    The title of 'perpetual curate' is now obsolete, having been merged with that of 'vicar'. Although Phillott held the living from 1808 until his death in 1851 he was non-resident throughout that period, appointing a series of assistant curates to perform his parochial duties. Such an arrangement was not unusual at the time.
4    WRO, BA924(4). Indenture re sale.
5    WRO, BA8474(2). Badsey Vestry Minute Book.
6    WRO, BA924(4). Will of Mary Collett.
7    WRO, BA924(6). Sundry documents relating to Bowers Hill Farm.
8    *The London Gazette* 31st October 1916.
9    EJ 5th January 1929.
10   WRO, BA5044(3). Poor's Land Accounts 1694-7.
11   WRO, BA8474(2). Churchwardens' Accounts.
12   Drift way : A road along which animals are driven to pasture or market.
13   Ordnance Survey Explorer 205 (1998).
14   *Rudge* = ridge. *Sellion* (or *selion*) = a portion of land of indeterminate area comprising a ridge or narrow strip lying between two furrows formed in dividing an open field.
15   Birmingham City Archives. MS3192/Acc 1930-009/362801.
16   Rev P Braby : Notes on Badsey and Wickhamford.
17   Wickhamford Manorial Book.
18   EJ 24th September, 15th and 22nd October 1927.
19   EJ 29th June and 6th July 1895.
20   Captain H F Stacke, MC : *The Worcestershire Regiment in the Great War*, page 413.
21   EJ 7th July 1934.
22   Shakespeare Centre Archive, Stratford-on-Avon, DR 165/565. Sundry documents relating to the Slatter family.
23   R W Sidwell : *A Short History of Commercial Horticulture in the Vale of Evesham* (Research Papers of the Vale of Evesham Historical Society, volume II, 1969).
24   Brian Kedward : *Angry Skies across the Vale* (1995).

## Acknowledgements

I am especially grateful to Mrs Maureen Spinks, who readily replied to my many requests for information regarding the Bowers Hill families. The staff at Worcestershire Record Office and at Evesham Public Library, where I made extensive use of the research facilities, were always most helpful. My thanks go to Mr and Mrs Martin Bent of Bowers Hill Farm, who supplied much useful information about the farm. Mr and Mrs J Ryan-Bell kindly allowed me to inspect the Wickhamford Manor Court papers and Mr Trevor Hockenhull provided some details regarding the Idiens family. I appreciate the help given by Mrs Janet Betteridge, who typed my original manuscript, and by my brother Patrick, who acted as proof reader. Finally, I thank my wife Sandra for her valuable support.

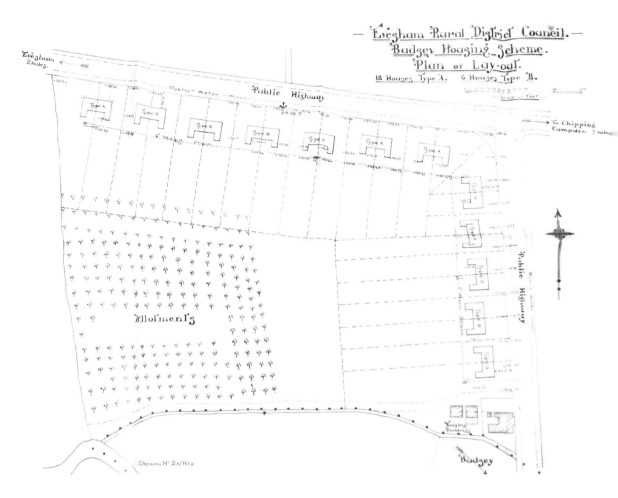

A plan showing the first 24 houses in Synehurst. The dotted line
along the lower edge of the plan marks the boundary between
Badsey and Aldington before 1921.

*One of the Synehurst houses today.*

# 3

# COUNCIL HOUSING IN BADSEY & ALDINGTON

## WILL DALLIMORE

It was a hundred years ago that the need for council houses in the village was first mooted. Badsey parish councillor, Charles Binyon, who was elected to Evesham Rural District Council in 1904, headed the call in 1909 for 24 cottages to be built under the provisions of the Housing and Town Planning Act. This act was brought in primarily to encourage cities to demolish back-to-back slum housing and replace them with more open council estates. In Badsey, Binyon's proposed cottages would eventually be built in Synehurst some ten years later. They were the first of over 270 council houses to be built in Badsey, 28 per cent of the village's current total housing.

Evesham Rural District Council (ERDC) was set up in response to the 1894 Local Government Act. Its duties included the provision of mains water and the disposal of sewage, plus the maintenance of the minor roads within its borders, which included the villages of Badsey and Aldington.

### Synehurst

The first world war interrupted Binyon's plans and they were put on the back burner until 1918. It is not known how the council decided on the location for these first council houses. Following the war the price of land slumped, which would have made it quite easy for the council to obtain land for building. The piece of land was known as Synehurst, near Badsey Pike. This name is a derived from the word Syne from the Seyne House, former name of the present Manor House, and the word hurst, which means rising ground.

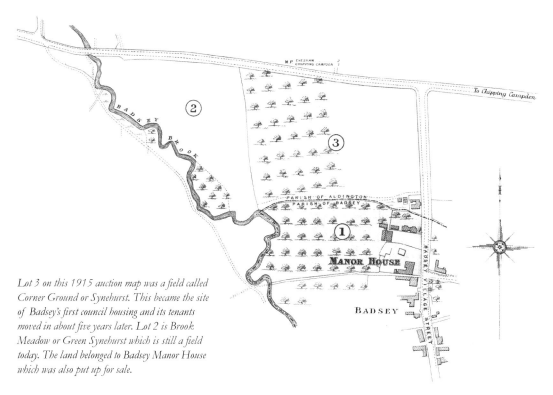

*Lot 3 on this 1915 auction map was a field called Corner Ground or Synehurst. This became the site of Badsey's first council housing and its tenants moved in about five years later. Lot 2 is Brook Meadow or Green Synehurst which is still a field today. The land belonged to Badsey Manor House which was also put up for sale.*

We do know that the council applied for a grant towards the cost of building the two dozen cottages. This was for £9800, which was around £400 per house. The houses were built in two styles, six with parlours, and the other 18 without. A parlour was what we would now call a sitting room. To describe these houses as cottages illustrates how much the word has changed over the years. These large dwellings of little or no aesthetic beauty are a long way from our perception of a quaint country cottage with a thatched roof. The one common denominator is that they were both built for poor rural folk. What Binyon saw at the turn of the 20th century was a village overflowing with horticultural workers and their families. The 1901 census shows that many houses were greatly overcrowded with generations of the same family. Their only salvation from this claustrophobic, unhealthy existence was that they could escape during the day into the open-air of the fields. It is no wonder when families were sought to occupy these first council houses that the demand was overwhelming, with almost 70 families vying for their tenancies.

By modern standards these first houses were pretty primitive. There was running water, but only cold water. To obtain hot water you needed to light a fire under the copper. This was a large open-topped cauldron shaped cast-iron vessel, usually built within the bathroom, or adjacent. A galvanised iron pipe would then lead from near the bottom of the copper to a tap located over the end of the white cast-iron bath. This was your hot water. In the houses in Synehurst these coppers were placed in what schoolboy George Geden, (who drew a floor plan of his council house for a school project in 1921) describes as a fuel store. This room would have held coal, and maybe wood and kindling. Coal fires were the only source of heating in the houses, not only the living room and parlour, but also in the bedrooms. One surprising fact is that the outside toilet was actually inside (see the plan opposite); something that was not repeated in council housing in the village until Horsebridge Avenue was built some 25 years later. The ground floor also contained a scullery, what we would now call a kitchen, together with a pantry, a store room, and a living room. In the living room was an open fire and to one side of the chimney breast was a built-in dresser.

The exterior walls of the houses had a rough-cast finish. This is a coat of cement render containing round stones applied to the nine inch solid brick walls and giving a weatherproof coating to the building. The reason this effect was used can only be guessed at. Possibly it was cost. Bricks were quite easy to obtain locally at the time with brickworks at Honeybourne and Evesham. Facing bricks, the ones usually used on the exterior skin of a building were traditionally dearer than the ordinary common brick, which would have been used at that time for the interior walls. Most of the private houses built at the same time used a red facing brick, so we know they were readily available. So why did the builders of the council houses not just use common bricks, without the rough-cast? The reason may have been that the majority of common bricks, especially from the Honeybourne brickworks, were semi-porous. They would not have withstood many winters without spalling, and if they were to opt for this cheaper solution then protection from the weather was essential. The rough-cast is effectively a raincoat for the bricks. A further thought is one of uniformity. ERDC was at the time building similar houses in many of the local villages. It would possibly have been easier and cheaper to apply the same building techniques to all comparable developments.

There is one downside to rough-cast houses and that is decoration. Without a spot of paint on the walls they look drab, cold and utilitarian, nothing like the image that Binyon was trying to achieve with his cottages. However, once paint has been applied, it is an ongoing process. Every ten years or so a new coat of masonry paint would need to be applied., not only to improve the looks of the building but also as protection from the elements. It was this type of maintenance which would lead

*Drawn in 1921, this sketch and plan show the new council houses built in Synehurst. The artists were two pupils at Badsey School: Charles Malin and George Geden. Charles's family were living at 3 Synehurst, on the left of the picture. Later George's family moved into 38 Synehurst, part of the 1927 development.*

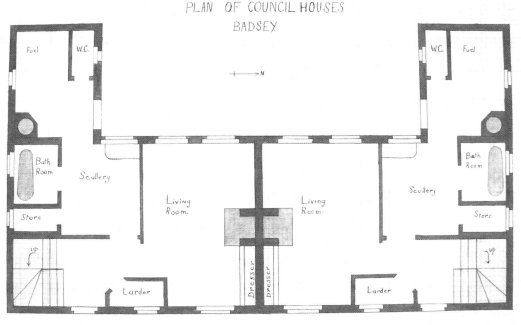

the ERDC to employ a direct-labour group of building workers.

With the houses came gardens. In the case of these first houses these were huge. The back gardens could stretch to 250 feet in length. Currently, the majority of front gardens are little more than overflow car-parks and back gardens put-down to lawns. Then the gardens were used more usefully. Fruit trees would have been planted, possibly at the bottom of the garden, under which chickens, contained in a wire-fenced pen, scratted. Vegetables would have occupied most of the remaining back garden with flowers being found in the front garden.

### The 1927 phase

In 1927 the next phase of council house building in Badsey was the construction of fourteen houses

*A 1931 plan of Synehurst showing completed houses and those being planned.*

on the east side of the Pike. The most northerly of these blocks of semi-detached buildings was placed just round the corner on to the Bretforton Road. At about the same time in Aldington eight houses of a similar design were built. Known today as Hillside, these would be the only true council houses built in Aldington. Another four houses were later constructed there in the 1950s but these were specifically occupied by senior members of the council and known as staff houses.

One of the differences between the Badsey and Aldington houses was the position of the outside toilet. In Aldington you would have to walk across the open back-yard, a concreted area the width of the house surrounded by a six-foot high close-boarded wooden fence, whereas Badsey residents only needed to take a couple of steps outside their back door as their toilet was built on to the house. Neither building was very inviting, although the whitewashing of the inside brick walls and sloping

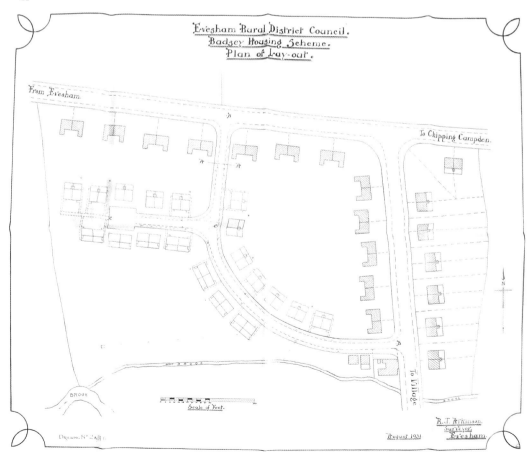

*Synehurst Crescent looking north in 2008.*

concrete roof made them presentable. The plumbing involved a high-level cast-iron cistern with a chain pull handle which flushed a cream vitreous-china pan. The wooden seat was possibly the only redeeming feature, but would be missed with the advent of the black Bakelite type plastic, which although more hygienic, was colder to the touch, especially in the winter. In fact it was the winter that found these outside toilets out. Unless some sort of heater, usually paraffin, was lit on a frosty night the lead pipes, however well lagged with Hessian sacking or newspaper, would freeze.

The council houses built so far had wooden sash windows. These were operated by either pushing up the bottom opening light so that it slid upwards in the rebated frame, or pulling down the upper light with a similar result. To compensate for the weight of the opening light and its panes of glass, an ingenious mechanism of cast-iron weights hung on sash-cords, concealed in the frame's housing, was used as a counter-balance, and helped with the opening of the window. The opening lights on the windows were often quite draughty and would rattle in the wind, and many a rolled-up sheet of newspaper was no doubt stuffed down between them each winter.

### 1931 plans

By 1931 plans were being drawn up for a further 38 houses in Synehurst. Eighteen of these would become Synehurst Avenue, and the other 20 form Synehurst Crescent. It can be assumed by the even spacing of Binyon's original cottages on the Bretforton Road that the proposed houses were never envisaged from the outset, as the gap between the council houses adjacent to the road is scarcely wide enough. This new housing scheme would also severely reduce the size of the large back gardens of the existing council houses which encircled the new site.

Neil Corbett lived in Synehurst Avenue between 1947 and 1967, here are some of his recollections.

"Inside the house, the kitchen was used as a general day room for meals, drying the

*47*

*Above: Evesham Rural District Council's Blackminster stores in 1968. The stores once stood on the corner of Birmingham Road and Station Road. The three large garages seen on the left housed the dust-lorries. The low buildings to their right were the foreman's offices, a toilet, wash-room and mess-room. The large buildings on the right were the stores and the carpenters' and plumbers' workshops. It was here on the 21st April 1965 that the author of this chapter, Will Dallimore, began his working life as an apprentice plumber.*

*Below: The ERDC logo.*

washing on wet days, ironing, and some food preparation. The kitchen walls were not plastered but were painted, and in later years papered. There was a fireplace in the kitchen and one 3 pin electric socket. The floor was originally red tiles, but later covered with lino. The pantry was separate from the kitchen, and a stone slab under the kitchen window would keep things cool. The sink was in the bathroom next door to the kitchen. The bath was covered by a board which was covered in Fablon and this also provided the equivalent of a modern kitchen work surface. The one sink tap provided cold water, and we had a gas fired Ascot heater to provide hot water. The sink was used for washing ourselves, the dishes, and sometimes clothes. Baths were once a week at most. We kept ourselves clean by washing at the sink. The bath was used for bathing and also for rinsing washing with Reckitts Blue. We had a copper which heated water for washing and baths. A gas cooker was also in the bathroom at the opposite end to the sink. Sometime around the late 1950s we got a Hoover washer-wringer, and soon after a spin drier. Next to the bathroom and under the stairs was the bogey hole. I suspect this was designed as a coal house but we used it for brooms, and general storage including sacks of potatoes. The front room was used most evenings to watch TV and for Sunday tea. There was a fireplace, and in the alcove to the left of the chimney breast was a built in dresser with two cupboard doors and two large drawers. There were picture rails around the room and on the floor, a large rug and polished tiles around the edge. The hall was only large enough to hang a few coats and open the front door (which was rarely used by the family). The stairs had a narrow stair carpet held in by stair rods, and painted wood either side. The largest of the three bedrooms was at the back of the house and had a fireplace which was never used. The windows provided little insulation and often iced up in winter. There was plenty of space for two single beds and other bedroom furniture. The larger front bedroom was big enough for a double bed and a wardrobe and a couple of chairs. In the smaller bedroom there was only room for a single bed and a wardrobe and a chair."

One subtle change by the architect, R J Atkinson, to these latest houses was in their appearance. Gone was the rough-cast exterior and its on-going decorating programme, to be replaced by pebble-dash, a cement rendering which had granite chippings thrown at it whilst the rendering was still wet. This effect provided the weather protection of rough-cast, but with the sparkle of the chippings affording the only decoration needed.

Another change from the previous council houses was the material used for the guttering. This was asbestos. Frowned upon now, but then it was a cheaper alternative to cast-iron guttering. The houses on the Pike and Bretforton Road had cast-iron guttering. This was in the form of six-foot lengths of four inch wide halfround gutter, bolted together with paint and putty as a sealant. The down pipes were six foot long and two and a half inches in diameter. They slotted together by means of a collar at one end. This collar also incorporated two ears as means of fixing the pipe to the wall, the pipe being secured by heavy steel pipe nails. The downside to this type of guttering was rusting. This could only be prevented by regular painting. The asbestos guttering was of a similar size to the cast-iron, but was lighter in weight, did not rust, and

never needed painting. It was bolted together using a bituminous sealant. The asbestos down pipes were fixed to the wall with a two-piece galvanised collar and bracket. One innovation of the time, which disappeared for many years, but has now returned, was the water-butt. A galvanised water-butt, or tank, was positioned, usually in the back-yard of the houses, to collect the rainwater from the down pipe. The tank was placed on two low brick piers, putting the tank at a height where the tap (opened by a quarter turn of the loose key handle) was high enough for a galvanised pail to fit under it. The tank also had a lid and an overflow pipe.

### 1945

The second world war interrupted council house building in Badsey, but by 1945 plans were being drawn up for over 70 houses to be built at Horsebridge Avenue. This market gardening land, known as the Hanging Ground, which despite its interesting title simply meant situated or lying on sloping land, was earmarked for development. This land, to the far north-west of the village, was originally in the parish of Aldington, but a re-drawing of the boundary in 1921 ensured that Badsey's neighbour had little say in what was built on the other side of the brook.

Around this time ERDC was also going through major changes. Within the next five years the office staff would move up Port Street, from number 64 to the newly acquired offices at Lansdowne. This was a large house opposite Bengeworth Church and had previously belonged to members of the Burlingham family. Meanwhile the manual staff would find their premises at Blackminster doubled in size. This involved the building of new garages for the refuse collection vehicles, cement store, offices for the foremen, toilet and mess-room. Blackminster stores, as it was known, housed two distinct groups of men. On the one side were those working under the council's banner of public health. These included the refuse collectors, the sludge lorry operators, and the gang. The gang consisted of around half-a-dozen men who were used in the maintenance of ditches, side-roads and other manual operations. The second group of men were on the building side; these included carpenters, plumbers, painters, bricklayers and labourers. They were employed to maintain the council's large housing stock. The stores, as its name implies, held a varied stock of building materials, everything from a tap washer to a tiled fire-surround, from a tin of the council's 'green front door paint' to various types of roof tiles. It also housed a joiner's workshop which fabricated windows, doors, skirting boards and mouldings. The stores was overseen by the store man. Harry Gould held this post for many years, a familiar figure as he putt-putted to and from his home at South Littleton on his moped. On his retirement Harry handed over the brown smock to Arthur Churchley who, having been employed as a bricklayer by the council, remained as storeman until his own retirement, not long before Blackminster stores was sold off and the site built on. Arthur, coincidentally, lived in the 1000th house to be built by ERDC, in Horsebridge Avenue, and the keys to the house were handed over at a ceremony on 26th April 1948 by the man who was instrumental in the building of Badsey's first council house, Charles Binyon.

## Horsebridge Avenue

By the summer of 1946 the circular concrete road of Horsebridge Avenue had been laid, with help from some remaining prisoners of war, amid the remnants of the crops and plum trees that still occupied the site. Compensation, to the total sum of £450, was paid to the market gardeners for these crops and the replacement of sheds and horticultural glass. A rather unsuccessful scheme in

*The photograph shows 31 Horsebridge Avenue and a ceremony in 1948 to open the 1000th council house built by Evesham Rural District Council. The Churchley family, who moved in, are in the middle of the picture. Mrs Churchley still lives there to this day. C A Binyon is the elderly gentleman second from the left. C H Gardiner is second from the right.*
*The Horsebridge estate consists of 74 houses (eight terraced houses, two detached houses and 64 semi-detached houses) built as an inner circle and outer circle. The inner circle was built first, in 1947, followed by the outer circle, taking about four years to complete. Mostly ex-servicemen moved into the new houses.*

*Buy and Bye: 38 & 40 Horsebridge Avenue in 2008. This photo illustrates how home ownership can radically improve a property. The house on the right was purchased in the 1980s from Wychavon District Council, and with the help of an improvement grant towards the cost of the 'bricking up', it has made the house not only more attractive but also saleable. Half of the Airey houses in Horsebridge Avenue have been given a new brick shell. All of these are in home ownership*

1947 by the ERDC to recoup some of this money foundered when fruit picked from the remaining plum trees realised only six pounds and sixpence when sold to Littleton and Badsey Growers.

Horsebridge Avenue marked a new era in the shape of things to come. In 1944 R J Atkinson, the council's architect and building surveyor, retired. He had been instrumental in the design of the majority of the council houses built in the previous 25 years. The future would see the emergence of architects such as Pemberton and Bateman who would incorporate new ideas and technologies into council house building. The first houses built at Horsebridge were the inner circle. They were built by Evesham builders, Wheeler & Mansell. These

32 red-bricked semi-detached houses had finally shaken off the curse of the Atkinson rendered wall, and emerged like red-admirals from their roughcast cocoons This was mainly due to the availability of a good quality, fairly cheap, facing brick. The London Brick Company was producing a range of bricks, including the Rustic, which was the type used at Horsebridge. The Rustic, little more than a combed common, was of a sufficient quality for the external walls, and with the advent of mass transportation, lorry loads of bricks could be driven directly to the site, and hand-balled into stacks adjacent to where they were required. Another departure from the previous nine inch solid brick external walls was the introduction of the cavity wall. Here the outer brick skin is separated from the inner skin, made up of 18 by 9 inch clinker building blocks, by a 2 inch gap. This air-gap was used as a barrier against dampness from the outside, and also gave a degree of insulation, although this would only be truly achievable years later when cavity-wall insulation became available.

The outer circle of Horsebridge Avenue contains

*A 1980 aerial photo looking north, with Bretforton Road at the top of the picture and Synehurst Crescent in the centre. The white masonry paint on the Synehurst houses makes them easy to identify. Two more recent council housing developments can also be seen. On the right of the picture is part of Green Leys built in the 1950s. The bungalows in the bottom left are part of Manor Close from the 1970s. Compare the size of the Synehurst gardens with those of the later houses.*

sixteen brick houses similar to the inner circle together with 22 Airey houses. Twenty-six thousand of these post-war prefabricated concrete structures were erected throughout the country as part of the Temporary Housing Programme between 1946 and 1955. They were manufactured by William Airey & Son Limited of York and some were put up for the council at Badsey and Middle Littleton by J C Meades of Evesham.

The houses did not require conventional footings and were assembled on a level concrete raft. A skeleton of the 4 by 2 inch reinforced concrete columns were placed at 18 inch centres to form the external, and central load-bearing internal wall. The exterior wall was formed by lapping 3 foot by 9 inch concrete slabs, hung from copper wires, to the columns. It is said that the one inch mild steel reinforcing tubes used in the columns were initially manufactured for use in the armaments trade but were surplus to requirements at the end of the war. Special floor joists, made from sprung steel wire

woven between two wooden battens, were bolted to the columns to form lateral stability. The roof was made up of pre-formed trusses, which carried concrete pantiles supported on laths fixed over a bituminous-felt membrane. The triangular gable end was partitioned and covered externally by lengths of 4 inch wide overlapping rough timber boarding fixed horizontally. A dividing wall of clay pot type bricks was built to separate each half of these semi-detached houses. There were three chimney stacks, a shared stack of two pots which was built against the dividing wall, and one further stack each, containing two pots, which were placed near the gable ends of the properties. There were two external doors to the properties; a main door on the side of the house and one at the rear. At the back of the house was a single-storey brick-built utility block. This housed a WC, a coal house and a wash house. The WC contained a white vitreous china WC pan with wooden seat, flushed from a high-level cast iron WC cistern with a chain pull. The cold water to the WC, and the adjoining wash house, was via a half inch copper service pipe. The coal house was basically of similar size to the WC The wash house contained a white vitreous china Belfast type sink sat on brick piers. Over it was a single cold-water tap. There was also a gas outlet for use with the free-standing galvanised copper boiler. The roof of the utility block was cast in concrete and covered with a bituminous felt. The guttering was 4 inch half round asbestos, which was also used on the main building.

The interior of the building was quite utilitarian. The ground floor contained a kitchen, living room, small sitting room and hallway. The kitchen included a pantry and a similar sized storeroom which housed the utility meters. In the living room was a cupboard for hanging outdoor clothes, the copper heating pipes running through the cupboard providing a degree of warmth. The living room also housed a built in three-drawer dresser with a two-door cupboard fixed to the wall above it. The first floor housed two good sized bedrooms, a small box room, and a bathroom. The main bedroom included a built-in wardrobe with a cupboard over the stair head in the box room.

The internal walls were foil-backed plasterboards nailed to wooden inserts in the concrete columns. Dado rails and picture rails were fitted to cover the joints between the plasterboards, due to the walls and ceilings not receiving a plaster skim.

The plumbing layout was of a design which would become the standard until the introduction of central heating in the sixties and seventies. A boiler, in this case housed in a range situated in the living-room, was heated by a coal fire, and the resulting hot water, with the help of gravity circulation, fed a copper cylinder in the upstairs airing cupboard. A cold water galvanised tank in the roof-space completed the plumbing system. The bathroom contained a white cast-iron bath, a white vitreous china wash basin, which sat on a cast iron cradle, and a white pressed-steel low-level toilet cistern. The soil stack was also unique in that it was housed inside the bathroom which avoided its waste pipes from freezing, as occurred on houses with external soil stacks.

Tenants later had the option of having their ranges removed from their living rooms to be replaced by a tiled surround and hearth, the cost of which would be paid for by the tenant. The council did however build a chimney breast and fit a back-boiler at no extra cost.

The windows of the Airey houses were also revolutionary. They were made of an aluminium alloy, which offered several advantages over the metal windows in the other houses in Horsebridge and those in Synehurst Avenue and Crescent. The original metal casement windows were made of steel. They were manufactured at a time when their coating was not to a standard of protection as were the galvanised finishes of later types. The main disadvantages were rusting and expansion. The expansion of the steel in relation to the glass could only be overcome by reducing the size of the panes, hence the original windows were made up of many small panes of glass and if regular decoration was not maintained then rusting would occur which led to the cracking of the glass.

## Play areas and the motor car

Horsebridge Avenue became the first council housing estate in Badsey to have a dedicated children's play area when a spare piece of ground in the north east corner of the estate was grassed-over and swings erected.

In fact grass figured quite large in Horsebridge, with continuous grass verges between the paths and road, and larger areas by the Remembrance Hall and bordering the 'top road'. The cutting of this grass became another of the council's duties, and a familiar sight for many years was Bill Dunkley of Aldington walking behind his Allen reciprocating sickle motor mower.

Children had previously used the roads and pavements as a playground, with the nearest street light becoming their meeting place, somewhere to tie a skipping rope, as a base for hide and seek, or its nocturnal equivalent 'tracking'.

The fifties heralded the emergence of the family car. Soon the streets and avenues would be filled with vehicles. Driveways and dropped-kerbs were installed, and the council embarked on a programme of building garages to rent. The first garages built were of brick construction with a pair of wooden doors. In 1952 a block of five garages was built in Synehurst Crescent on the site of an electrical shop, which had previously been a fish and chip shop. These garages would however themselves be demolished when the entrance into Manor Close was opened-up in the late sixties. In 1954 four garages were built in Horsebridge Avenue, with a further ten built several years later which occupied part of the children's play-area. The swings did survive this initial encroachment, but not for long, as they were removed to make way for a block of concrete garages. These modern garages, with their

54

up-and-over metal doors, and corrugated asbestos roofs were the shape of things to come. However these first half-dozen would be pulled down in the 1980s to build Packs Close.

## Green Leys

In 1954 the council obtained a compulsory purchase order on an old orchard owned by Lucy Wheatley, which was to become Green Leys. The name is a historical reminder of its proximity to Badsey Leys and Badsey Green. Fifty dwellings would be shoe-horned into an area barely half the size of Horsebridge Avenue. This claustrophobic concept could only be achieved by reverting back to the use of terraced housing and a drastic reduction in the size of the gardens. Another modern concept was the laying of a large grey paved area, known as 'the slabs', which acted not only as a walkway but as the only safe place where a child could play. The one concession to aesthetic taste in Green Leys was in the choice of the bricks used for some of the houses. The architect included a straw coloured brick from the London Brick Company's Chiltern range.

By this time the demography of the council tenant was changing. Previously most council houses were built with three bedrooms, suitable for established families with children, or for young families to grow into. The council recognised that there was a need to provide accommodation for tenants who fell outside this criteria and so eight flats were included in Green Leys, as well as some

*Above: Box clever: 35 Green Leys in 2008. This is one of a block of council houses in Green Leys. Its square lines and plain brickwork well match our perception of the archetypal council house.*

*Below: These residents of Green Leys had something to smile about when this picture was taken in 2005. Not only was their road 50 years old, but they had all lived there for 50 years and had each celebrated at least 50 years of marriage. They are Mike and Joyce Hewlett (No 2), Lionel and Rene Guise (No 5), Bernard and Joan Hewlett (No 8), Len and Pat Lord (No 20), Des and Iris Syril (No 22), Roy and Mary Page (No 28), Glan and Muriel Williams (No 37), outside No 22. John and Margaret Collett, Chris and Bet Hall and Helen Stanton had also lived at Green Leys for 50 years but are not pictured. Visiting granddaughter, Brittany Page, sported a Local Heritage Initiative T-shirt along with granddad Roy.*

two-bedroom houses.

The relationship of council house tenants with horticulture was also declining. Whereas the majority of the early settlers who moved into Synehurst and Horsebridge were employed on the ground, this was now changing, and the age of the commuter was upon us. Many villagers were bussed to work at Cheltenham, Tewkesbury or Long Marston and new and emerging job opportunities would allure school-leavers away from following their parents on to the land.

## St James Close

In the early sixties, the council, having filled the top left-hand quarter of the village with houses, plunged into the heart of Badsey with a controversial decision to compulsorily purchase Wheatley's Orchard. The main objection was that it meant the removal of an old horse-chestnut tree which stood alongside the Green Footpath and had supplied conkers to children for years. Its compatriot horse-chestnut book-end which stood on the corner of Brewers Lane and High Street, was saved, and survived until 2008. St James Close, so named due to its nearness to the village's church of St James, included 24 houses, with white painted fences, grassy banks and a modern fresh look.

Every new council estate built was an improvement on the last, both in comfort and amenities. This meant that the older council houses in Synehurst were being left behind with this progress. Improvements to these properties over the years had been piecemeal and basic. The repeated coat of paint, new tap washer or pane of glass had been the most the council could offer. As time went on tenants demanded more. The hardboard boxed hot-water heaters that sat in the corner of a bedroom or perched on a pair of angle-iron brackets in the bathroom were scant substitute for the contemporary centrally heated semi.

It was in the late sixties and early seventies that ERDC embarked on a massive improvement scheme to bring their older council houses up to date. These conversions, carried out by the council's own building staff as well as local building sub-contractors, meant tenants enduring several weeks living in caravans sited in their front gardens. The work involved the removal of the original downstairs bathroom and the area opened up to provide an enlarged kitchen. Plaster was applied to the walls, fluorescent lights to the ceilings, and kitchen units sat beneath Formica work tops. Where possible long bedrooms would be split to accommodate the new bathroom. Alternatively, bathrooms would be added in houses by means of a ground floor extension. New plumbing and electrical wiring was included with centrally-heated radiators provided in all rooms, fuelled by either solid-fuel or gas boilers.

## Manor Close

Manor Close was Evesham Rural District Council's final foray into council house building in Badsey before being swallowed up by Wychavon District Council in 1974. The name of the road, for it technically became a road when it was linked to Seward Road, is from the nearby Manor House, on whose land part of it sits. This housing estate best illustrates the requirements of council house needs at that time. Many of the existing three-bedroomed council houses were occupied by elderly couples. They had brought up their families there, but their

children had long since flown the nest. The houses were too large for them, and would be better suited to a younger family group. So Manor Close sees more than half of its housing as bungalows, ideally suited for the retired person or couple. The rest of the site is made up of semi-detached and terraced houses.

These were not the council's first bungalows in Badsey as they had previously built three in Old Post Office Lane, and a pair beneath the surviving horse-chestnut on the corner of Brewers Lane. Incidentally, one of the bungalows in Manor Close was the 2000th council house to be built by the ERDC. It was built by Wheeler & Mansell, the same builders who built the 1000th council house in Horsebridge Avenue 34 years earlier.

## Right to buy

The Housing Act of 1980 gave tenants the 'right to buy' their council houses. Large discounts, depending on length of occupancy, ensured many potential homeowners found this an offer too good to refuse. A short term mortgage, or even a cash payment, was preferable to paying years of rent. Rules were however applied to enable the council to recoup its discounted sale price should the property be resold within a 5 year period. It was then just a matter of the new owners 'de-councilising' their property. Rough-cast walls

*Style Council: 18 & 19 St James Close taken in 1968. The arched hoods to the front doors, and the white painted railings typify 1960s style. The large windows and single chimney stack are clues to the presence of central heating, an essential part of modern living.*

PHOTO: L W TAYLOR

PHOTO: VIRGINIA PAWLYN

*Old Folks at Home: 32, 34 & 36 Manor Close photographed in 2008. Towards the end of the sixties it became apparent that housing was needed specifically tailored to the ageing population. Manor Close saw the first, and last, massed group of council bungalows built in Badsey.*

changed colour overnight, double glazing replaced old sashes, plastic fascia concealed rotting joist ends and tarmac drives were carpeted with coloured bricks. Some of the owners of the Airey houses in Horsebridge Avenue combined the 'this is not a council house' philosophy with the realisation that the reselling of their houses would be difficult in its prefabricated state, so the cladding of them in a brick skin has ostensibly killed two birds with one stone.

Packs Close, a group of eight dwellings, tucked away in the corner of Horsebridge Avenue, and falling under a new concept known as 'social housing', was one of the last housing projects built in Badsey by Wychavon.

By the mid-eighties Wychavon District Council decided to close Blackminster stores. The house maintenance, carried out for may years by its direct building staff, was contracted-out. The refuse collectors and their lorries were relocated to Evesham, and the contents of the stores auctioned off. Lansdowne offices were sold and turned into private apartments. In 1994 Wychavon handed over its remaining stock of council houses in Badsey and Aldington to the Evesham and Pershore Housing Association.

What of the future? Well, we may have seen the last of the 'true council houses'; the large avenues and closes. Before Charles Binyon visualised his cottages, the only rented accommodation was through private landlords. And this is possibly what we are heading back to, whether it is the housing association with its infilling programme, or the developers attaching a few social housing dwellings to their private schemes. We may never witness again the scale of council house building that has been undertaken in Badsey in the last hundred years.

### Acknowledgements

I am grateful to everyone who has provided information and ideas for this chapter. The ERDC plans and papers are held by the Worcestershire Record Office.

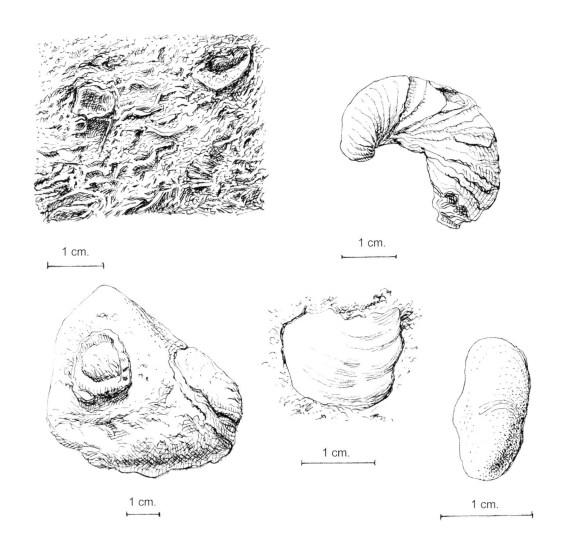

1 cm.

1 cm.

1 cm.

1 cm.

1 cm.

*Fossils found in local stone fragments.*
*Clockwise from top left:*
*Densely embedded remains of small clams and crustacean parts.*
*'Devil's toenail' found loose in soil.*
*Mussel-shaped bivalve.*
*Flat clam shell.*
*Cockle-like bivalves embedded in a stream pebble.*

*All the illustrations in this chapter were drawn by the author,*
*Ian Gibson.*

*Cottage in Aldington built mostly of Littleton stone.*

# 4

# BADSEY ROCKS: LOCAL GEOLOGY & LANDSCAPE

## IAN GIBSON

Rocks have been studied for thousands of years for the treasures they contain. They have provided gems, minerals, metal ores, coal and building stone since the beginning of human technology, but the organised scientific study of geology is a relatively young subject. It was only in 2008 that the 150th anniversary of the founding of *The British Geological Association* was celebrated.

In the Vale of Evesham the underlying rocks are well hidden by recent soil sediments but until the last century there were several quarries along the road from Badsey to the Littletons.

In this part of Worcestershire the closest rock to the surface is the Lower or Blue Lias. This is a sedimentary rock made up of layers of soft clays and hard bands of flagstone. Both are blue grey in colour. Although the word 'sedimentary' does not sound that exciting, rocks of this type are the best for revealing the secrets of life far in the distant past when conditions were very different to the present day. Fortunately our local Blue Lias rocks are richly endowed with fossils which have a fascinating story to tell about a very different world long ago. In more recent times the effect of the geology on human activity in the Vale of Evesham has been significant and worthy of consideration.

When one passes a local garden or house wall which is constructed of locally quarried Blue Lias there is no obvious sign of any fossils, just some fine horizontal banding rather like the lines of pages in a closed book seen end on. Actually there are very abundant fossils compressed in this rock but they are hidden just like the words are hidden in a closed book.

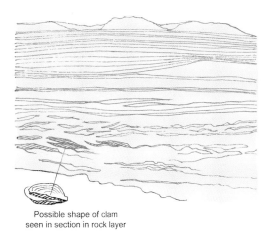

Possible shape of clam
seen in section in rock layer

*View of flat broken edge of Littleton stone showing banding of
Lower Lias sediments and shell fragments seen in section.*

The analogy of comparing geology to a book is worth pursuing further. It has been said that the layers of rock that make up the geological sequence are like the pages of a book and the fossils are the words. This book about the evolution of life is open in our part of the world at a fascinating chapter when big changes were afoot.

## A tale of two layers

If you were to dig a deep hole in the soil in the Badsey area you would be likely to end up with a well, as the water table is high in this area with many streams draining the Vale into the River Avon. So after fixing up a pump to keep the excavation free of water the observer would notice that for several metres down there would be relatively soft material consisting of layers of clay and gravel. Below this however there would be a sudden change to a greyish coloured rock which would be seen to occur in thin layers alternating between harder and softer beds with many small fossils present. Of course the hole could be made deeper to uncover other kinds of rock representing earlier and earlier periods of the Earth's history.

The top layer of soil, clay and gravel is no older than the last Ice Age, that is, about 8,000 years ago. Immediately below this however the grey rock formation contains fossils that are 200 million years old. This poses the question—what happened to all the layers in between?

This chapter aims to help explain this and also reveals how, at the time our bedrock was being laid down, great world geological events were happening on the surface of the planet.

## Starting at the Bottom

The oldest fossil bearing rocks in Britain go back an unimaginable 600 million years. Our local rocks go back a third of that distance in time to the early Mesozoic Era. This Era started with the Triassic period 245 million years ago when the world was dominated by a huge land mass or supercontinent known as Pangaea, which ran from pole to pole across the equator. The only modern continent it would have resembled would be Australia but Pangaea was many times bigger and it would have been even hotter and drier in the interior. At the end of the Triassic period forces deep within the Earth caused Pangaea to break up. Parts of the super continent sank and, along these lower areas, rifts began to form separating parts of the supercontinent into new smaller land masses that would be recognisable in shape today. These new huge land masses were to become the continents we are now familiar with such as Africa, North and South America and Asia. The rocks that were to become southern Britain had been in the centre of a vast desert for 45 million years but were now at the edge of one of the new rifts that were letting in the sea. They were on the edge of what was to become the continent of Europe. This meant a dramatic change from desert conditions to a new landscape of salt water lagoons and encroaching sea. Of course these changes didn't happen overnight – they took a few million years to become noticeable. But in terms of the planet's history, this was a quick change, so marked that geologists have identified this time, 208 million years ago as the boundary between the Triassic and the Jurassic periods, the latter period perhaps being better known as the beginning of the *age of the dinosaurs*. The last Triassic sediments were reddish sandy sea water deposits now known appropriately in our part of England as *Mercia mudstones* but as the seas grew deeper the sediments changed to fully marine deposits of soft calcareous mud that would over enormous lengths of time transform into grey limestone, the Blue Lias. The rocks of Badsey are right at the bottom of the Lower Jurassic which is exposed along a relatively narrow stratum, or layer,

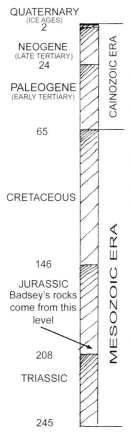

QUATERNARY
(ICE AGES)
2

NEOGENE
(LATE TERTIARY)
24

PALEOGENE
(EARLY TERTIARY)

65

CRETACEOUS

146

JURASSIC
Badsey's rocks
come from this
level

208

TRIASSIC

245

CAINOZOIC ERA

MESOZOIC ERA

*Geological sequence from Triassic to the present (in millions of years).*

of rock running from Lyme Regis in Dorset northeast to the Humber Estuary.

From this broad picture there are many details which can be filled in. Geology has been mentioned as a recent science. In fact the first person to draw a colour coded map of British geology was one William Smith (1769-1839). He did his training as a mining surveyor in Stow on the Wold and started his career on the Somerset coalfield. Subsequently he worked on the construction of canals, which were being dug all over the country in the late 18th century, as the industrial revolution took off. This unique experience gave him the insight that the layers, or strata, of British rocks followed a consistent pattern that could be drawn up into a map. He also noticed that most of the rock strata tilted down to the southeast corner of England. His remarkable coloured map was first published in 1801 and is very similar to the modern version available today. Naturally as a British genius he was not recognised as such until late in his life after enduring hardships and a period in a debtors' prison.

## Pangaea and Plate Tectonics

Badsey, as Pangaea broke up, was about 2000 miles further south, close to the equator and immersed under several hundred metres of sea.

To explain how this state of affairs came about it is helpful to go back even further into the geological past.

As early as 1596 the Dutch map maker Abraham Ortelius noticed how the coast lines of West Africa and of North and South America looked as though they could fit together. Over the succeeding centuries all sorts of theories were devised to explain what came to be known as *continental drift*. The evidence that the modern continents were once in contact with each other began to stack up. Striations, left by ancient glaciers which would be expected to flow from the poles in the direction of the equator, have been found lying in various directions suggesting that the underlying landmass had been rotated over time. Evidence was also found in the way ancient magnetic fields had been trapped in the rocks. The fossil and living evidence consistently showed similarities between populations living near the boundaries of the existing continents that once fitted together into a much larger entity known as a super continent. The German geologist Alfred Wegener introduced the theory in 1912 but he could not suggest a viable theory for a mechanism for the vast forces that could produce such movement.

It was not until the deep exploration of the ocean beds in the 1960s that the mechanism was discovered. Along the centres of the Atlantic Ocean lines of volcanic activity were discovered along rifts in the ocean floor. It was realised that new ocean floor was being made and the continents each side of the rifts were being pushed apart as if on a conveyor belt. The actual reason this happens is still not clear, but the science of *plate tectonics* was born, and at least it is agreed that the continents are situated on larger chunks of the earth's crust, known as *plates*, which are pushed across the globe by currents in the molten magma below. There appears to be variation in these forces, described

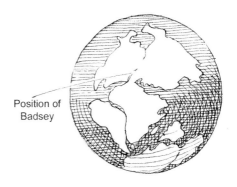

Position of
Badsey

*The Earth at the beginning of the Jurassic period showing the break up of Pangaea.*

as heat flow, acting from deep inside the planet, so that there have been relatively stable periods when little movement happened, followed by increased heat flow from beneath causing new movements to start up.

For the preceding 40 million years Pangaea had been home to evolving land animals. This was a great age for the early reptiles, which could cope with the hot dry conditions. Modern reptiles are still most common in the hotter parts of the world. There was a long period of expansion and evolution producing reptiles which were the ancestors not only of the dinosaurs but also the branch which became the ancestors of the mammals. In fact a late fossil from the Triassic shows impressions of bristles around the nose, hair being an essential mammalian feature.

As the super continent started to break up, climatic conditions would have altered substantially as inroads of the sea occurred, creating new oceanic currents and making weather cooler and wetter. Badsey has bedrock that is very close to the boundary of this world changing transition: it is only necessary to travel to Windmill Hill, South Littleton, to reach the nearest Triassic bedrock. Taking the footpath from the nature reserve on the hill to the Fish and Anchor pub by the Avon one can see, whilst crossing just one freshly ploughed field, the transition from buff coloured soil at the top of the hill (Jurassic) to reddish coloured soil at the bottom (Triassic).

The Earth's fossil record has shown, that at certain points over the immense period that it has taken for life to evolve, strange events, called *mass extinctions*, have happened. At these times unusually large numbers of plant and animal species disappeared, never to return. Palaeontologists, looking for fossil evidence of life after the cataclysm, found small numbers of surviving species in higher (later) strata. Higher still, these survivors started to increase in numbers and produce variations which in due course gave rise to new species. After a few million years the recovery of life was substantial but made up of new types. There are generally agreed to have been five of these major extinctions and one of them happened at the end of the Triassic with up to 35 per cent of living families (large groups of related species) dying out. Controversy always surrounds the causes of mass extinctions and so it is not entirely clear whether the big changes in climate caused the event or whether it was something else that happened at roughly the same time. There were two large meteor impacts 210 million years ago, in Western Australia and Quebec, Canada. The cause might have been similar to the one which, it has largely been agreed, finished off the dinosaurs and many other species at the end of the Cretaceous 66 million years ago, when a large meteorite crashed into the Gulf of Mexico.

What is certain is that the world was changing profoundly at the end of the Triassic. Increased activity in the magma under the Earth's crust was putting a strain on the giant continent of Pangaea and something had to give. Huge fissures began to appear and sea levels around the world started to rise. The dry desert conditions that had dominated the land were gradually changing. The last rocks laid down in the Triassic were the Mercia mudstones created from the calcareous mud of freshwater lagoons that were proliferating and which in due course were to sink below the rising sea waters.

## The Bivalve Bonanza and the Dawn of the Decapods

Following on from the changes happening at the end of the Triassic period, the continents we know today were beginning to separate. Vast lengths of new coastline were forming along the cracks as the continents separated. The gaps filled with water from the ocean to create shallow seas where there had previously been barren deserts. Shallow coastal seas are very rich environments for marine life because of the warm temperatures and the abundance of nutrients coming in from rivers. This tends to encourage phytoplankton to multiply in the surface waters and, as they become the fuel for the food chain, all the other organisms benefit. Shellfish had been around for a long time before the Jurassic period but this increasing area of sea floor created massive opportunities for numbers to shoot up and for new species to arise in order to fill the various niches in the developing ecosystem. So at the start of the Jurassic, the scene was set for an explosion of sedentary molluscs, expanding in diversity and numbers. They were the bivalves, with bodies enclosed and protected by two valves or shells, and the gastropods, with the body coiled

*Ammonite and ichthyosaur – Jurassic sea predators.*

inside one twisting shell.

However all this tasty seafood lying around on the bottom presented an irresistible opportunity to predators. Fish had been around for a long time but their jaws were not bony enough to be very strong. The thick bivalve shells were perfectly adequate to protect their owners. The new situation drove evolution onwards relatively quickly and new species of fish appeared with jaws powerful enough to get at the bivalve flesh. Other animals were getting in on the act too. The early Jurassic also saw the first crabs (the decapods) with crushing pincers, while other molluscs, such as whelks, were evolving the means to bore holes through the once impenetrable shells.

This sustained attack on the bivalves did not wipe them out – they are not exactly rare today. The way they survived was to evolve several strategies to avoid predation. Mussels retreated up the beach to grip exposed rocks by means of strong threads glued to the substrate, and thus became inaccessible to crabs and fish while the tide was out. Most species developed long siphon tubes so they could sit deep in the sand below the reach of attackers, while still being able to bring down fresh water and food to be filtered. The giant clam evolved huge size as a defence while the razor shell feeds at the surface of the sand while being able to shoot downwards

quickly by means of its long foot, held at the bottom of its burrow. The scallop famously and atypically for a bivalve, uses speed to avoid capture, as it can lift off the bottom and swim backwards by flapping its shells like old fashioned false teeth.

A local speciality that can be spotted when walking by freshly ploughed fields in Badsey is Gryphaea arcuata, an oyster like bivalve that must have been extremely abundant in the early Jurassic. This fossil is so well known as to have the common name *devil's toenail* because of its claw like shape. They used to be collected and ground up to be added to cow feed. The calcite they are made of would have helped cattle bone development. It is impossible not to marvel at this 200 million-year-old fossil when you hold it and see the clear growth rings marking ancient seasons.

**Meanwhile in the Seas above**

Large predators swam in the waters above this arms race in the silt and mud. Well known today is the ichthyosaur, a dolphin shaped air breathing reptile. Fossils of this two metre long sharp toothed hunter have been found in Worcestershire quarries. As with modern whales and dolphins there were several species, adapted to feed on different types of fish and other prey. These aquatic reptiles evolved from ancestors which had lived on land earlier in the Triassic period. Some of their relatives had to come ashore to breed but the ichthyosaur lived its whole

# What was the shape of the Triassic Landscape?

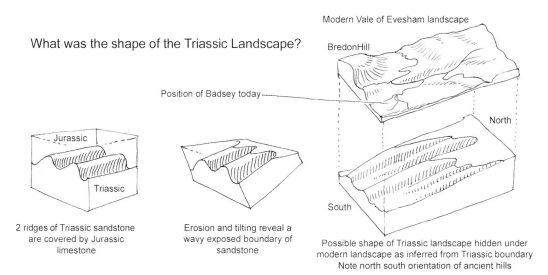

Modern Vale of Evesham landscape

Bredon Hill

Position of Badsey today

North

South

Jurassic

Triassic

2 ridges of Triassic sandstone are covered by Jurassic limestone

Erosion and tilting reveal a wavy exposed boundary of sandstone

Possible shape of Triassic landscape hidden under modern landscape as inferred from Triassic boundary Note north south orientation of ancient hills

life at sea. Fossils have shown that the eggs hatched and were retained inside the mother so that miniature adults were released, able to swim and feed independently from birth.

The ammonites were a very widespread group of predators, variable in size from a few centimetres to over a metre in diameter. The body plan was like a coiled squid with an external shell. The ammonites belonged to the cephalopod group of molluscs and their spiral fossils are very recognisable. Large numbers have been discovered in the eroding cliffs around Lyme Regis. They controlled their buoyancy by altering the amount of gas stored in their shells and swam slowly catching small prey in their tentacles. The close relative, the nautilus, still lives in the deep ocean in parts of the Pacific region, coming to the upper waters under cover of darkness to feed while safe from attack itself. The ammonites went the way of the dinosaurs at the end of the Cretaceous period. There is increasing evidence from the change to more oddly shaped and armoured shells that ammonites were already under pressure from shell crunching fish species before the event that caused their mass extinction. It is thought that the different reproductive strategy of the nautilus saved it from extinction. It produces few eggs but these are protected by the adults at depth, whereas the ammonites mass spawning created vulnerable young which did not survive the carnage in the upper waters.

Our Badsey bedrock was being laid down at the time these events were taking place. As time passed

more sedimentary rocks were deposited above this layer and so it became hidden as the book of geology got thicker. These events will be given some explanation shortly in this chapter but it is worth pondering on the thought that at the time and place of Badsey today we have the book of fossil history open at this page. But as pages are constantly being added or torn away, at another point in geological time the page on view would be quite different.

## Names and Colours

It is worth having a look at the question as to why the Lower Jurassic rock is called *Blue Lias*. The blue description comes from the presence of tiny particles of iron disulphide, better known as iron pyrites. This mineral is well known as *fool's gold* after its glittering metallic yellow colour. At a microscopic level however light is scattered so as to appear blue-grey. Most of the fossilised clay is made up of very fine particles of silt and the accumulation of the remains of the protective calcareous exoskeletons of surface phytoplankton. The origin of the name Lias can be explained at this point. It is not derived from a geographical location as so many geological names are but is actually derived from quarryman dialect pronunciation of 'layers'; hence 'liayers'; hence 'lias'.

Triassic sandstone is red because it was formed in desert conditions where ferric oxide built up in the wind blown sand. The fine (0.5 mm - 2 mm) clear quartz grains worn spherical by the constant friction against other grains became cemented together by ferric oxide which is a major component of rust, therefore giving the reddish colour.

## The Missing 200 Million Years

In a word the answer to this riddle is erosion. But in order for rock to be eroded it has to be laid down in the first place. The geological record shows that amazingly for much of the following 140 million years southern Britain remained submerged at varying depths under the sea. A brief summary is therefore required of the main events of more than a third of the Earth's history since the dawn of complex life at the end of the Precambrian period.

The main reason for the rise in sea level at this time was the opening of the rifts in the new oceans. Upwelling of magma under the small but widening stretches of water had the effect of pushing up the Earth's crust and raising sea levels around the world. Pangaea was breaking up so that the deep ocean around the separating super continent became shallower. Running north to south down the centre of the young Atlantic, the North American plate was splitting away from the European plate. Along this split, molten magma from deep under the Earth's crust pushed up to drive the process of separation. This upwards pressure actually created a tilt in the tectonic plates so that they sloped downwards away from the split. It can be inferred by analysing the composition of the rocks what sorts of conditions were prevailing at the time of deposition. Over the millions of years following the end of the Lower Lias, complicated climatic changes and variations in sea level produced the deposition of distinctive beds of rock above the

Lower Lias but still within the Early Jurassic group of rocks. Imaginatively they are known as the Middle and Upper Lias. Both of these outcrop part of the way up Bredon Hill but have been eroded away in the Vale of Evesham. At Bredon, the Middle Lias is given the name marlstone. It is particularly rich in iron and in other areas has been mined as a source of iron ore.

Conditions changed again at the end of the Early Jurassic as carbonates, concentrated in shallower water, were precipitated in the form of tiny egg shaped particles, building up cream coloured limestone strata called inferior, and later, superior Oolite. Higher iron content in some of the deposits created a yellower rock now famous as the Cotswold limestone.

Sea levels remained high for most of the rest of the Jurassic period, and so more rocks were deposited, such as the richly calcareous Cornbrash and sandy Kellaway beds. Meanwhile things were happening in the North Sea which were significant enough to deserve their own section, so that follows next.

## An Oil Story

C H Gardiner[1] described problems with water mains in some parts of the Vale of Evesham because of the corrosive nature of some of the subsoil. A water pipeline installed to connect Badsey to Pebworth Reservoir kept leaking due to excessive corrosion. This pipeline ran via Blackminster and Cow Honeybourne to Pebworth. In 1937 an engineer's report recommended the use of asbestos pipes to replace the original iron ones. The corrosion occurred when the pipes ran through patches of

*Position of the bedrock of Badsey over time since the early Jurassic.*

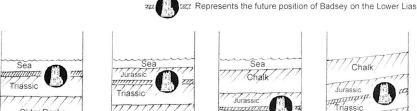

acidic black sticky subsoil. Similar black bituminous subsoils occur around Kimmeridge in Dorset. Here it is a sign of oil measures which outcrop in the cliffs along this part of the coastline. Rich oil bearing rock is exposed at the surface and the adjacent 'nodding donkeys' of the Wych Farm oilfield are testament to a small but worthwhile supply of 'black gold'. The exposure of Jurassic formations along a diagonal axis from Dorset to Humberside has already been mentioned and they pass through our region. This actually continues out under the North Sea towards Norway and the oil and gas fields there have been exploited for the last 40 years or more. So do we have oil under Badsey? In order to answer this question a bit of background is necessary.

After the Jurassic, tectonic movements pushed up a land mass in the area now occupied by the North Sea, but due to the development of faults around this region it later slumped to form a large basin which subsequently filled with sediments. Instead of being fossilised as rock, plant and animal remains became trapped in pockets and their decomposition produced deposits of concentrated hydrocarbons. The North Sea oil and gas fields were being created. Over millions of years these pockets were subjected to high temperatures and extreme pressures under hundreds of metres of later sedimentation in a complicated process which concentrated the hydrocarbons but also shifted them across the faults into earlier layers which were now at the same level, such as the Great Oolite stone of the mid Jurassic. The systems producing

this effect are known as *oil kitchens* and modern day oil prospecting involves discovering these large accumulations of oil and gas deep under the seabed.

To return to Kimmeridge, the closeness to the surface of the oil-bearing rock has made this small oilfield a viable concern.

So is there oil under Badsey? Alas or fortunately depending on your point of view, it is very unlikely. To form oil bearing measures the Great Oolite of 170 million years ago was not thick enough for oil kitchens to form in Worcestershire. Also in our area it has all been eroded away, taking any oil with it but leaving odd patches of acidic bitumen like those mentioned by C H Gardiner.

### After the Oil

The Jurassic finished 146 million years ago to be replaced by the great age of chalk, the Cretaceous period. In our area it began with a drop in sea levels, but when the sea eventually returned, the water contained levels of algae that reached very high densities. The remains they showered to the sea bed contained a particularly pure form of calcium carbonate which fossilised to produce chalk. The Cretaceous lasted 81 million years so the chalk accumulated to depths of hundreds of metres.

The Cretaceous had another characteristic which changed the landscape. There was a return to instability in the Earth's crust and so many volcanoes appeared, even one in Holland. So as well as the bed of the Atlantic Ocean getting wider, southern Britain was subjected to squeezing from

*The position of the Lower Lias in England compared to a liquorice allsort.*

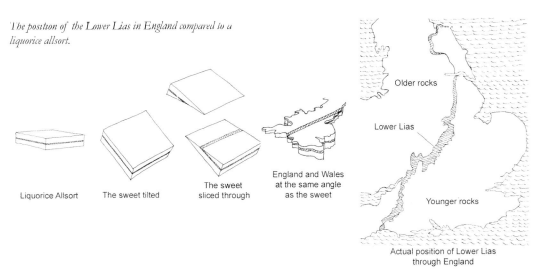

Liquorice Allsort        The sweet tilted        The sweet sliced through        England and Wales at the same angle as the sweet

Older rocks

Lower Lias

Younger rocks

Actual position of Lower Lias through England

the collision of Africa with southern Europe. The Tethys Sea which had been ocean sized in the Jurassic period almost disappeared, to leave the comparatively small Mediterranean, still shrinking today and subject to frequent volcanic eruptions. The net effect of this on southern England was to tilt the land down to the southeast and to throw up hills such as the Chilterns and the North and South Downs which run mainly east west.

As the northern parts of the country rose out of the sea, erosion started to remove the Cretaceous chalk. This erosion has continued since the dawn of the *age of mammals* 66 million years ago when the ammonites, ichthyosaurs, dinosaurs and in fact 70 per cent of known species vanished at the rather abrupt end of the Cretaceous. The erosion which started then is continuing today so that hundreds of metres of limestones and chalk in the Vale of Evesham have been worn back to show us a snapshot of early Jurassic marine life that is represented by our Lower Lias.

## The Ice Effect

We are now up to about 2 million years ago which compared to the 200 million years old Lower Jurassic sounds quite recent, but the landscape here would not yet be recognisable. Badsey if it had existed then would have been a Cotswold village! This is because there were dozens of metres of Mid Jurassic Cotswold Stone still to be worn away to reveal the rocks Badsey is built on. The steep slopes of the Cotswold edge which is now above the village of Broadway was then several miles further north. A process was however just about to start which would cause erosion on a grand scale. The Ice Ages were here.

Opinions differ on how many Ice Ages there have been since the beginning of the Quaternary Period 2 million years ago but there have been at least nine cold periods when the arctic ice sheets have spread over Britain causing the characteristic scouring of northern valleys by glaciers. Some ice sheets came as far as Worcestershire and as they retreated they left behind deposits of ground up rock originating from further north. The legacy of this today is that there are considerable variations in acidity and subsoil types over quite small distances. For example just south of the Bretforton Road the soil is littered with fragments of mid Jurassic Cotswold stone

washed down from the Cotswold edge in the fierce river erosion that happened as an ice age ended. A short distance to the north of the road the soil is virtually free of stones and consists of orange brickearth, created by accumulations of loess, or wind blown dust, characteristic of the tundra conditions close to an ice sheet during a glacial period. In a field next to the plot now occupied by Cotswold Garden Flowers in Sands Lane the soil is alkaline one side of a ditch, yet acidic on the other side. Some of the clay encountered when digging locally may not be Blue Lias but boulder clay, another deposit left by the retreat of glaciers. In the Vale of Evesham some of the worst erosion happened at the beginning of warm periods when torrents of meltwater etched the surface into wide valleys. The damage was amplified by the action of boulders crashing along in the flow. Harder tables of Cotswold Stone resisted the destruction longer and so we have hills such as Bredon and Dumbleton, with hard caps of mid Jurassic stones. The underlying soft clays of the Lower Lias will eventually ensure the destruction of these hills, as the softer clays erode more quickly so as to undermine the limestone hillsides. Every now and then this causes the edges of the hill to collapse in the form of landslips. The tilting of Britain was halted during the ice ages due to the enormous weight of the icecap pressing down on northern Britain. Water trapped as ice was lost from the seas resulting in lower sea levels so that during each glacial period Britain became reconnected to the mainland of Europe.

This brings us to present times where, 8000 years since the last Ice Age, modern soils have been created out of a combination of erosion products from the ice ages and the build up of organic matter from past vegetation.

## Recent times: the Influence of Geology on Human Activity in the Vale

The underlying bedrock has an inevitable influence on the landscape through the effect on the soil and the shape of the land surface. To discover the uses that have been made of the Lower Lias one has to look at the development of the chief activity of this region, agriculture and horticulture. To grow good crops a decent soil is essential. From Iron Age times the Vale soils have been known to produce excellent cereal crops. Local archaeologists believe that the Romans built several access roads in this area to improve the transport of wheat grain to Ryknild Street which ran south from Yorkshire through the West Midlands via Studley and Alcester and then on to Stow on the Wold where other roman roads connected to the channel ports. Stoneford Lane in Bretforton is thought to be part of a Roman Road which ran from a junction with Ryknild Street at Honeybourne, then across south of Badsey at Pear Tree corner and on past Wickhamford to Hinton Cross where it may have continued under the present A46 to what is now Cheltenham.

After the end of the Roman period cereals remained an important crop into medieval times. Mixed farming with the open field system developed and the long narrow field shapes associated with this survived into the early 19th century when the old boundaries were recorded in several parts of Badsey at the time of the enclosure survey.

The easiest land to be worked became the centre of settlement so it was inevitable that the most successful farms were built in what became the centre of Badsey and also Aldington.

The soil here is friable loam which is light to work and easily accessible. The closeness to Badsey Brook explains this. Alluvial silt from periodic flooding has left a rich deposit of light fertile soil. Today much of this land has disappeared under modern housing which gave a better return to the farmers than growing crops. The old farms have survived as some of the more substantial old buildings such as Seward House, Aldington Manor and Harrington House. At Seward House the narrow private road which runs off the High Street past Sladden's Barn was once the access lane to the farm lands with barns and other farm buildings sited along it.

Further out from this nucleus of settlement the soil is much more influenced by the Lower Lias clay. This had two conflicting qualities. The calcareous Lias clay produced a high level of lime which was a very important constituent for its ability to grow good crops. However the thick clay in the soil mixture made it heavy and hard to work. In the days of ox and later horse ploughing cultivation was so tough that farmers described fields as 'four

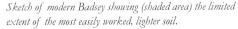

*Sketch of modern Badsey showing (shaded area) the limited extent of the most easily worked, lighter soil.*

68

horse' or 'six horse' land according to the proportion of clay in the tilth.

Large areas were set aside for orchards which had the advantage of producing a valuable crop without the need for constant ploughing. The increase in intensive market gardening was another development which exploited the fertile soil to produce crops such as onions and beans. This made the hard work of cultivation more cost effective. In the late 1800s asparagus and other high value crops were introduced and the development of the Evesham Custom[2] enabled tenant gardeners to pass on their plots for substantial sums. So the richness of the soil won out over its stubbornness to plough and Badsey became a valuable and innovative centre of production. This change from conventional farming to market gardening was the main reason for a doubling of the population of Badsey in the 20 years from 1891. These interesting changes in cultivation and population show just how important the underlying geology can be to the historical development of an area. The softer beds of Lower Lias have influenced the soils but the harder beds of rock have had a significant effect too.

It is hard to imagine now but in the not too distant past there were quarries in our area. The main ones were situated along what is now Birmingham Road, running north to Blackminster and The Littletons. This is no coincidence because this road runs along a north south ridge of harder bedrock which has resisted erosion and marks the eastern edge of the Avon flood plain. The local rock is very close to the soil surface at South Littleton. Small chunks litter the fields after ploughing and can easily be seen from the public bridleway connecting the village to the Windmill Hill Nature Reserve.

W Pitt, writing in his book on the agriculture of the area, published in 1813, mentions that he had found quarries in North, Middle and South Littleton. At South Littleton he saw a lime kiln in operation 'where lime is burnt for manure'. It is possible that the location for this quarry was on the south side of Station Road. In 1866 this land was called Quar Ground in a sales document.

There were several good reasons for digging stone in these local quarries. Pitt gives useful details. He described the rock as a hard calcareous flagstone, large quantities of which were used for gravestones,

barn floors and domestic floors in kitchens and halls. The flags were about 80 mm thick and could be obtained in a wide variety of lengths some up to 4 metres. It could be bought by the foot length at 5d per foot. Broken pieces and stone waste were also important. They were used for mending roads but also for burning in kilns. The high levels of calcium carbonate in the rock would have been exposed to high temperatures in the kilns to produce lime which was an essential soil improver for acid sandy soils. For example members of the brassica family such as cabbages and cauliflowers do badly in acid soil. The red sandy soils further north in Worcestershire were improved by the addition of lime so it is no surprise that the stone from these local quarries became so well known it was widely referred to as the Littleton stone. Lime was also a major ingredient of lime mortar used for building construction.

The other use is what remains today as the most visible sign of the local geology. The older buildings in Aldington and Badsey show extensive use of the thick slate like slabs of Littleton stone where it is used as infill and boundary walling. The corners and window surrounds of such buildings as Harrington House are made of dressed oolite, the well known honey coloured Cotswold stone brought over from quarries above Broadway or in some cases from the ruins of Evesham Abbey. This gives a neat smooth finish to the building with courses of cheaper unworked flags of local Littleton stone making up the plain walls in between. Even at the site of Evesham Abbey, although the surviving Bell Tower is constructed entirely of Cotswold stone, Littleton stone was used for the boundary walls and The Almonry as well as extensively in the churches of All Saints and St Lawrence. As one approaches St James in Badsey from the High Street the church seems to be built entirely of Cotswold stone but actually this applies only to the tower and the extension of 1885. From the other side, most of the stone work is of the humble Littleton stone.

The reason the old quarries are hard to spot is because they have been developed, usually as business premises, so that Badsey's quarry is now beneath the farm buildings currently occupied by the Vale Garden Centre at Blackminster. This quarry was still visible as a hole in the ground within living memory. Further up the road, the Blackminster Business Park is located in the buildings formerly used by Littleton and Badsey Growers and Cadburys. This land was previously a redundant quarry. The first house recorded there was built in the 1840s for the foreman of the stone quarry. The census records for Blackminster reveal that men were involved in stone working until the beginning of the 20th century. In 1851 Edward Powell was a foreman for the stoneworks and lived at the first house in Blackminster, the old farmhouse. In 1861 the house was occupied by the stone mason Thomas Moore and his family. Subsequently the activity seems to have changed to lime burning, perhaps as local demand for building stone had diminished with the increasing popularity of bricks for house building. In the 1871 census Thomas Lansbury was recorded as a quarry labourer but he lived in Badsey so may have worked at the quarry further south where the Vale Garden Centre now operates. A business directory of 1873 records that a Lime and Stone Works at Blackminster was owned by George Hunt of Bridge Street, Evesham, but there is no record of a resident stoneworker in Blackminster until 1901 when Rose Cottage was occupied by Charles Heywood, a limeburner, with a large family. The cottage had been built before 1871 and previously occupied by an agricultural worker. George Hunt died in 1917 and it seems the works ceased to be run after this date. The lime kilns were behind the site of Harvards which has itself recently been demolished.

In Warwickshire, the town of Rugby, also on the Blue Lias, became the home of Rugby Cement, a major manufacturer. With the advent of cheap transportation by rail in the Victorian era and the mass production of cement and fertilisers, the local producer would have ceased to be economically viable and the quarries and kilns became redundant. Nowadays, in order to build using the local type of Lias stone, it is necessary to import a very similar stone from quarries in Somerset such as Ham Hill or Ashen Cross, as much of the county lies on the same bedrock as Badsey.

## Conclusion

Our local rocks give an insight into a very different world in the distant past. The story of the geology of Badsey and Aldington is a continuous tale of sea level fluctuations and the effects of sediments being laid down, turned to rock then being worn away. Spread over 200 million years this all happened very gradually and the process is still going on right now. After the recent occurrences of serious rain water flooding in the Vale of Evesham it is quite a thought to consider that for over three quarters of the time since the Triassic, Badsey was submerged beneath the sea.

## References

Gardiner, C H 1937. *Extracts from a report by A. J. Atkinson.*

Gaut, R C 1939. *A History of Worcestershire Agriculture and Rural Evolution.*

Hoggard B 1998. *Bredon Hill, a guide to its Archeology, History, Folklore and Villages.*

Institute of Geological Sciences, 1979, *Geological Map of the United Kingdom, South 1:625,000*

Pitt, W 1813. *General View of the Agriculture of the County of Worcestershire with Observations on the means of Improvement.*

Sidwell, R W 1963. *A Short History of Commercial Horticulture in the Vale of Evesham.* Research Papers, Evesham, 2

Toghill, P *The Geology of Britain, an Introduction.*

## Notes

1  *Charles Henry Gardiner* is the subject of another chapter of this book.
2  The Evesham Custom is described in chapter 4 of *A Brief History of Badsey and Aldington,* second edition, by T C Sparrow, Badsey Society, 2002.

## Acknowledgements and disclaimer

I am indebted to my wife Lynn for proof-reading, to Jane Neill for the details of C H Gardiner's observations and to the Badsey website for the transcribed census information. I cannot claim more than an amateur interest in geology and local history so while I have tried to avoid errors this introduction should not be taken as by any means definitive. Indeed it would be good if this chapter encourages any reader with local knowledge to come up with more information on this topic.

*Careful examination of these two 1884 photographs of Badsey churchyard provided important clues about stones that were missing or had been moved.*

*An aerial view of the churchyard today.*

# 5

# 'HERE LYETH' IN BADSEY CHURCHYARD

## PETER STEWART

My interest in churchyards and monumental stones began some 34 years ago when I started researching my family history and that of my wife who was born in Badsey. In the earlier years, family history was in its infancy, as were computers which today provide the family historian with many sites full of information. However, these websites do not have all the answers, in particular where people were buried.

In the 1980s and 1990s, Worcestershire churchyards and graveyards were surveyed by teams of people, all volunteers from the Birmingham and Midland Society for Genealogy and Heraldry (B&MSGH). The published results are available from that organisation.

However, I decided that an independent survey of Badsey churchyard was needed in view of the fact that the original burial registers were not consulted by any of the teams, nor were stones cleaned, nor those lying face down turned. This was due to restrictions in force in 1987. I found a large number of inscriptions incomplete, and numerous discrepancies between the inscriptions and the original burial registers. I was soon to learn never to take for granted what was written on a monument. There are many examples: two people being in the same plot, the husband who died at an early age, his wife who remarried and chose to be buried with her first husband, both being in the index under the first husband's name. Sometimes a married daughter was interred with parents and again being indexed under the father's name. This is not the fault of the researcher as the stone only showed 'wife of', or 'daughter of'. The published survey by the B&MSGH for Badsey contains 443 monumental inscriptions with an index of 776 names, and contains maps showing locations of the monuments, including those in the church interior. Some of the inscriptions are no longer readable and therefore this remains an important document. In July 2001 I decided to carry out a new and independent survey of the Badsey monuments and burial registers, and to provide a photographic record of the monuments before some of them deteriorated any further. My survey of the churchyard is ongoing to ensure that each new headstone is photographed and the inscriptions recorded. Monumental inscriptions appear on gravestones, headstones, ledgers, memorial tablets and plaques.

### The Burial Registers

Before recording the inscriptions relating to interments, the church burial registers were first consulted, including those held on microfilm in the Worcester Record Office (registers 1 to 3) and those presently held by the incumbent (registers 4 and 5). The Bishops Transcripts were also examined, and a number of burials not recorded in the registers were found and added to the burial database. There are five burial registers covering the following periods:

Register 1 contains 1520 burials from 1538 to 1784. An additional seven burials were found in the Bishops Transcripts, and two omissions.

Register 2 contains 207 burials from the 16th January 1785 to the 23rd December 1812.

Register 3 contains 801 burials from the 12th February 1813 to the 8th September 1906. This register appears to be complete, however, there are no burials recorded for 1882 in this register. The burial registers of nearby Wickhamford were also consulted, but no burials were recorded there in 1882 for Badsey residents.

Register 4 unfortunately has a large number of omissions from 1936 - 1947, including all after March 1936 up to early 1945. Some missing burials, from May 1942 to 1947, have since been added to, or inserted on paper between the pages of the register, by a later incumbent. I have been able to add a further 77 omissions to the list after reference to the monumental inscriptions, verbal information from surviving relatives, and from reading the obituaries in the *Evesham Journal and Four Shires Advertiser* for the years 1936 to 1945, copies of which are held

on microfilm in the Evesham Public Library. Including 106 known omissions, I have recorded 863 burials from the 9th October 1906 to the 20th November 1968.

Register 5 contains 578 entries from the 7th December 1968 to the 12th April 2008. In addition two recent interments of ashes in family plots have not been recorded in the registers.

### The Book of Remembrance

This book, covering the period May 1964 to July 2000, is kept in a display case inside the church. It contains the names and dates of death of 117 individuals whose cremated ashes were interred either in the Garden of Remembrance, or elsewhere in the churchyard, or another cemetery (one known individual). The names of 33 of those listed are also recorded in the burial registers. The ashes of one individual were interred in a family plot in Evesham.

### The Survey

The survey[1] was carried out as intended, with each monument personally examined and the details on each recorded, including the type of monument. Details were recorded on paper and electronically on a computer. All stones lying face down were lifted and read, and the bases of part sunken headstones and kerbs were also uncovered and checked; and in doing so, revealed some unrecorded inscriptions of individuals and verses. The ground was thoroughly probed over a period of weeks, and seven previously unrecorded 17th and 18th century stones were uncovered, including three out of place footstones belonging to nearby headstones. An examination of the 1884 photographs of the churchyard (reproduced at the start of this chapter) revealed more footstones than were found during this survey, most matching up with headstones commemorating interment of members of the Byrd families. All the headstones shown in the photographs are now lying flat in the grass. With digital enlargement I was able to identify some of these footstones and connect them with known parent stones. However, despite a thorough search, these footstones have not been found. Either they have been damaged and removed, or buried beneath their parent stones. The second 1884 photograph shows three monuments. The two stone crosses to the right of the picture mark the graves of Frances Mary Warmington, and of Mary and William Parker. Both these monuments are still in their original positions but now badly eroded, that of Mary Warmington totally, and that of Mary and William Parker partially. The cross on the left of the picture commemorates the interment of Robert Henry Hambler and his three children Sarah Ann, and twin sons Robert Henry and Frank George. This stone is still in its original position but lying flat. Robert Hambler was a farmer who originated from Colwall, Herefordshire, and his wife, Elizabeth, who is not buried in the churchyard, originated from Powick in Worcestershire. Mary Elizabeth, their surviving daughter, married George Field, a farmer, in Badsey in 1869.

The oldest stone uncovered in the churchyard is dated 1644. This headstone commemorates the death of Elizabeth George who died on the 26th of February of that year. Other George family stones are located nearby. One footstone, inscribed 'I P 1663', caused some confusion at first, as no

*A footstone marking the burial of Jane Pigeon in 1663.*

*The oldest stone uncovered in the churchyard, dated 1644.*

75

PHOTO: PETER STEWART

*This 17th century footstone bears only an inscribed verse, obviously relating to a female interment, but as there is no accompanying headstone, the identity of this lady will never be known.*

individual with these initials was buried in that year, only a Jane Pigeon. However, a bit of research into 17th century handwriting revealed that the letter J and I were often interchanged; therefore our footstone belonged to Jane Pigeon who, according to the registers, was buried on the 20th of May 1663. This footstone has no parent stone, though a totally eroded headstone lying face down and close by is the most likely candidate. Another 17th century footstone bears only an inscribed verse, obviously relating to a female interment, but as there is no accompanying headstone, the identity of this lady will never be known. Both this and the above mentioned 1644 stone are in an excellent state of preservation, and for this reason have been covered over again with turf.

Some stones are large and undoubtedly very heavy and make one think of the problems the stonemasons encountered in transporting them and placing them *in situ*. The Ballards from the Littletons, the Gardiners from Evesham and, from Badsey itself, the Crisp family are some of the stonemasons' names to be found inscribed at the foot of many of the earlier headstones.

There are references to Crisps as stonemasons in the census returns for Badsey, beginning with the 1841 census. Stephen Crisp was baptised in Holy Cross Church, Pershore in 1787, the son of Mary. He married Elizabeth Falkener in Badsey in 1813. Stephen's grandson Elijah was the first postmaster of Badsey. He and his family were to run the village post office for some 60 years. Considering his sons were stonemasons, it is somewhat surprising that there is no monument to mark the last resting place in Badsey churchyard for Stephen Crisp or his wife Elizabeth. She died in 1845 and he in 1858.

The more informative stones and commemorative plaques will be found inside the church where people of importance and wealth are commemorated. Some were actually buried in the chancel inside the church. The stones set in the floor have been worn by centuries of feet passing over them and have become much less legible than those on the walls. The inscriptions on old stones in the graveyard have suffered far worse in many cases. The weather has affected the earliest gravestones, especially those made of the local stone where some have crumbled leaving no trace of what was carved there. Those lying flat with the inscription uppermost have suffered most from the weather, and fallen debris from the trees above, as well as being trodden upon by numerous passers by. Clinging ivy has also destroyed the faces of a number of stones, particularly when it is pulled off.

When one strolls through the churchyard, it is hard to believe that, according to the records, some 4095 individuals have been interred herein since 1538; though with omission in the registers and unrecorded interment of ashes into family plots the number is probably nearer 4200. Prior to 1538 we have evidence of burials in the chancel thanks to Evesham historian E A B Barnard[2]. These two come from wills he read –

*Clinging ivy has destroyed the faces of a number of stones.*

Margerie Smythe of Badsey: 'My body to be buried in the Chancel of St James (undated, probably 1534).

John Smythe of Badsey: 'Body to be buried in the Chancel of Saint James Church' (Feast of St Egwin Abbot, 1535).

The last resting place of less than a third of those interred in the churchyard has been found during my researches. A number of those buried there appear in my family tree; therefore I can put some faces to the names on the headstones. Others I have known personally at work, or have obtained photographs of. I have a photograph of William Mustoe who died in August 1944 at the grand old age of 102. Another picture of him appears in the local book *The Vale of Evesham: A Pictorial History*. The oldest individual, whose ashes are interred in a family plot, is Helen Gertrude Hartwell (née Stampe). She died on the 5th February 2002, just thirteen days short of her 104th birthday; outliving

her husband, Elgar Thomas Hartwell, by 33 years. Her parents, Herbert Ernest and Louise Eliza Stampe, died in the 1940s. Slightly younger when they died were Louisa Malin (née Moore), at 100 years old in 1910, and Claressa Alice Richards at 102 in 2001; both outliving their husbands by 22 years and 31 years respectively. A short note, based on an interview with Louisa Malin by an Evesham Journal reporter in 1910, will be found in *A Brief History of Badsey and Aldington* and her obituary appeared in the November 1910 issue of the Parish Magazine.

There are also 106 individuals in the burial registers whose ages range from 90 to 99 years old. Sadly there are many interments of those who did not enjoy a long and fruitful life. One 18th century headstone informs us that Thomas and Mary Bird lost four children, including twins. They were aged

*Four little faces worked in relief across the top of the headstone for the children of Thomas and Mary Bird.*

from just seven weeks to six years old[3]. There are four little faces worked in relief across the top of the headstone for this family. As mentioned above Robert and Elizabeth Hambler lost three children, all in their infancy in the 19th century. John and Clara Jelfs lost three children, aged between three weeks and 17 years old between 1883 and 1900, but the last resting places for these three, and many other children interred in the graveyard, are not known. While the commonest name in the burial registers is Knight, with 174 recorded burials from 1561 to December 2003, the surnames of Brzezinski, Knurek, Olender and Tyszkow are less so, and reminders of the war years, and the arrival of foreign refugees into the region when the war ended; a number of them eventually settling in Badsey and becoming part of the village community. The surname Rosskopf is particularly interesting. Johann Rosskopf was a World War I German prisoner of war, who was billeted in Badsey Manor House, and died in November 1918 at the age of 33 years. His remains were exhumed in 1963 and removed to the German War Cemetery at Cannock Chase[4]. The name Willi Ritterswuerden is also commemorated in the graveyard. He was a German prisoner from World War II, who decided to remain in England after the war. He married a local girl, Evelyn Major, who now lives with her daughter in America.

As an exercise and for a future talk I blindly selected a headstone in the churchyard in order to find out the ancestry of those interred in the plot.

My selection involved a headstone dedicated to Fred and Margaret Kate Cleaver (née Brailsford) who were married in Badsey church in 1941. Fred Cleaver originated from Bretforton, but a long search of many registers and census returns revealed that his line of Cleavers originated from Oxfordshire; his 3x-great Grandfather Joseph Cleaver being a shepherd in the village of Steeple Barton in 1788. Fred Cleaver's uncle, another Fred, is also interred in Badsey churchyard along with his wife Edith Mary (née Jelfs). They were married in Badsey church in 1928.

My researches also cover the churchyards at Bretforton and Offenham as well as the council controlled graveyards at Bengeworth, Hampton and Waterside[5]. I derive great pleasure in recording inscriptions and the photographing of the many varieties of memorial stones. I also enjoy my talks with the people I meet in the various locations. I learn of their lost family members and something of their past, often interesting and bringing the various names on the memorials to life, be they a butcher, baker or candlestick maker, but market gardener and agricultural labourer are the most common occupations encountered locally, particularly in Badsey. The occupations of the deceased here are not recorded in the registers, and very few occupations can be gleaned from the memorials. Some only give a name and the date of death, while others do offer more – date of birth, relationship to another person, such as 'wife of' or 'daughter of'. Often, as several people are buried in the same grave, there will be a whole string of connected people listed, some with different surnames – all good stuff for the family historian. Some list the actual house or farm where they lived and some are inscribed with the military rank they held, particularly on the war graves. Two stones tell us that William Bell was for 20 years farm bailiff to A H Savory of Aldington Manor and that William Barnard was for 50 years Clerk of the Parish. However, one has to look at the obituaries in the Parish Magazine to learn a bit more about William Barnard:

> "He was also for a long series of years village postman, and his duties in this connection brought him continually into Evesham, where he made many friends, and where he was a familiar figure. He was of small stature and very spare, but a man of wonderful vitality, and at the advanced age of four score years could walk as briskly as many a man not half his age. On one occasion, in his eighty-third year, he walked to Evesham and back three times, and later in the day went to Malvern and ascended the Worcestershire Beacon."

*Modern headstone for Fred and Margaret Kate Cleaver.*

*Stone, with cross missing for William Bell, farm bailiff to A H Savory of Aldington Manor.*

One inscription which caught my attention and seemed worthy of further investigation involved a Richard Knight who 'met his death by accident, April 15th 1891, aged 26.' I was surprised to learn that Richard was employed as a labourer on the Manchester Ship Canal Works. He was one of 16,000 men and boys working on this project. He was at work in the Eccles cutting and became caught between a steam working navvy and the rock face. A navvy is a large steam-powered excavating machine, an early power shovel. The accident was witnessed by his brother who was working within a few yards of him. Richard died of his injuries the following day, one of many men who died whilst working under brutal conditions on this project. Richard was unmarried, the son of Richard and Jane Knight (née Mowbray).

I feel it would be more interesting to include the occupations of the deceased on memorial stones rather than the lengthy endearments one comes across these days. All too often one finds the words 'never to be forgotten' on long neglected graves, when perhaps 'once blacksmith of this village' or 'retired post master' would be more informative. Though, one is mindful of the extravagant cost of burials which limits what is inscribed on the stones today. However an occasional amusing verse would not go amiss as can be found elsewhere where there are stones inscribed 'Beneath this Sod lies another' and 'She always said her feet were killing her but nobody believed her.'

*The author, Peter Stewart, conducting field work in Badsey churchyard.*

PHOTO: RICHARD PHILLIPS

## Notes

1 The results of the survey are published on the Badsey website www.badsey.net – and in book form as *St James Church, Badsey, Worcestershire, A survey of the Burial Registers, Interments and Monumental Inscriptions* by Peter Stewart, July 2002. A copy is deposited in the reference section of the Evesham Public Library.

2 Evesham historian Mr E A B Barnard FSA contributed notes on some *Old Badsey Wills* to the 1913 edition of the Badsey Parish Magazine and these are reproduced on the website www.badsey.net. This was part of Barnard's research on the history of the Rural Deanery of Evesham. The wills are now in the Worcestershire Record Office. Those quoted are *Cal. Worc. Wills,* Vol I, p 7, fs 32 & 35.

3 The Bird family also lost another child, Samuel, who died in 1750, at the tender age of two years and eight months. His burial is not recorded in the Badsey, or any other local register, and is probably an omission.

4 See *The Seyne House* chapter in this book for more about the German prisoners of war at the Manor House.

5 Some of this work is deposited in the reference section of the Evesham Public Library.

## References

Badsey Parish Magazines – 1898-1978.

Child, Mark 1982. *Discovering Churchyards.* Shire Publications Ltd.

Cramp, John 1981. *Discovering bells and bellringing.* Shire Publications Ltd.

Dale, W L, 1946 (2nd ed.) *The Law of the Parish Church.* Butterworth & Co, London.

Farmer, G, Boaz, J, Bushell, L, Lawley, G and Page, P 1987. *Monumental Inscriptions, St James Church, Badsey, Worcestershire.* Published B&MSGH.

Fletcher, Ronald 1980. *In a Country Churchyard.* Granada Publishing Ltd. Paladin Books.

Jeremiah, Josephine 1997. *The Vale of Evesham, A Pictorial History.* Phillimore & Co.

Lees, Hilary 1993. *Hallowed Ground, Churchyards of Gloucestershire and the Cotswolds.* Thornhill Press.

Lindley, Kenneth 1972. *Graves and Graveyards.* Local Search Series. Routledge & Kegan Paul, London.

Mytum, Harold. 2000. *Recording and Analysing Graveyards.* Practical Handbook in Archaeology 15. Published by the Council for British Archaeology, in association with English Heritage.

Rayment, J L 1981 (3rd edition). *Notes on the Recording of Monumental Inscriptions.* Federation of Family History Societies.

Rayment, J L 1992 (4th edition, revised by Penelope Pattinson). *Rayment's Notes on Recording Monumental Inscriptions.* Federation of Family History Societies.

Redgrave, Sam 1992. *Here lyeth the Body …A look at Worcestershire churchyards.* Halfshire Books.

Seaman, R D H and Sparrow, T C 1983. *A Brief History of Badsey and Aldington.* Published by the authors.

Sparrow, T C 2002. *A Brief History of Badsey and Aldington.* Second edition. The Badsey Society.

The Badsey Society 2002-2008. Newsletters Nos. 1 – 24.

White, Leslie H 1987. *Monuments and their Inscriptions, a Practical Guide.* Society of Genealogists.

## Acknowledgements

While the reading, recording, cleaning, and photographing of the inscriptions involved only myself, the whole project would not have been possible without the help and encouragement of others, and for this I give my thanks to the following: the Reverend Dr Adrian Hough, and more recently the Reverend Richard Court, for the freedom they allowed me to carry out this survey, and access to the burial registers in their care. For their work on the original 1987 survey I thank the team of volunteers from the Birmingham and Midland Society for Genealogy, namely Pauline Page, Linda Bushell, Geoff Farmer, Jeremy Boaz and Gillian Lawley. The Staff at the Worcester Record Office and the Evesham Public Library were always welcoming and helpful during my visits, for which I thank them also. Thanks are also due to the following: John Bolton (Bell Tower Captain), Hilary Bolton (Ringing Master), Sue Cole, Roger Savory, Terry Sparrow, and Church Wardens, Chris Robbins and Chris Smith. I also acknowledge the help I received from brothers John and Will Dallimore and David Caswell. David provided many interesting facts regarding persons interred in the graveyard. My thanks also to all the visitors and villagers I have met, or corresponded with, during this survey, for the interest they have shown and continue to show in my activities, and for the useful information I have learned from them during our conversations. My final thanks are due to Maureen Spinks and Richard Phillips, for their continued support in my activities and again to Richard for the excellent way he has presented my work on the Badsey web site.

*The only known photograph of the Aldington Mill complex which appeared as a postcard in the early 1900s.*
*The mill building is central, with living accommodation in the foreground. The engine house is on the left, storage barns on the right and mill house behind. The gable end of the workshop block with a dovecote can just be seen to the left of the mill house. The mill pond is in the left foreground. Two people stand on the right of the picture, one apparently white with flour.*

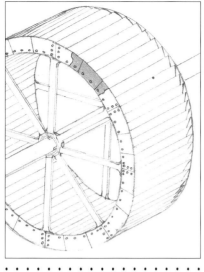

Part of Aldington waterwheel as it might have looked.

# 6

# ALDINGTON MILLS

## MIKE LOVATT

"Behind the house an old walled garden, with flower bordered grass walks under arches of honeysuckle and roses, gave vistas of an ample millpond at the lower end, forming one of the garden boundaries. The pond was almost surrounded by tall black poplars which stretched protecting arms over the water, forming a wide and lofty avenue extending to the faded red brick mill itself, and whispering continuously on the stillest summer day. The mill wheel could be seen revolving and glittering in the sunlight, and the hum of distant machinery inside the mill could be heard. The brook which fed the pond was fringed by ancient pollard willows; it wound through luxuriant meadows with ploughed land or cornfields still farther back. The whole formed a peaceful picture almost to the verge of drowsiness and reminded one of the 'land in which it seemed always afternoon'."

This extract is taken from the book *Grain and Chaff from an English Manor* by Arthur Savory who was the tenant farmer living at Aldington Manor from 1873 until 1901. He wrote this book about the village after he retired to Hampshire. It eloquently describes the watermill, which is the subject of this chapter, and which was such a central feature of village life, whether as a place of employment, as a source of business, as a place for mischievous boys to play, or just as a place to sit or lie beside on a sunny summer afternoon.

An attempt has been made to piece together what we know of the buildings, business and people of Aldington Mill, a way of life so different from ours now in such a relatively short space of time. The mill is still within living memory, but only

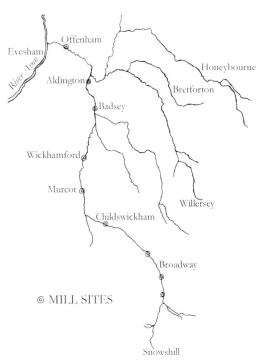

Above: A sketch of the Badsey Brook and other local brooks showing the known watermill sites.
Below: A photograph of the ancient Faulk Mill at Offenham in 1903, showing the dilapidated state the mill had reached. This is typical of small country mills of that era and it can be seen it would have been easier to demolish it than repair. The building was demolished around 1920.

just: it seems important to record what we do know for future generations.

## Brooks and watermills

Aldington is fed by two streams both of which carry water from the western slopes of the Cotswold escarpment.

Badsey Brook rises near Snowshill and flows through Broadway, Childswickham, Murcot, Wickhamford, Badsey, Aldington and Offenham all of which had or have watermills.

Other streams flow from the north of Broadway through Willersey and Bretforton and, joining a stream from Littleton and Blackminster, flow into Badsey Brook just north of Aldington.

From Aldington the combined brook meanders to Offenham before flowing into the Avon near the Bridge Inn.

There were three mills at Broadway, two corn mills and one which was a silk mill at some stage in its life. Upper Mill was located on the Snowshill Road, the next at Bury End, nearer to the village, and the third, Lower Mill on the Winchcombe Road. Childswickham had a corn mill near St Marys Church, now converted to a house. A corn mill at Murcot is shown on a 1905 map.

Next is Wickhamford Mill which is largely unaltered, then Badsey Mill[1] which started life as a corn mill and was extended and converted to a silk throwing mill by 1818. Nothing remains of the 19th century mill itself. Aldington Mill was next downstream and finally Faulk Mill at Offenham which still existed in 1905 but nothing remains today apart from a fine mill house.

The only mill which is still complete is Wickhamford. A certain amount of restoration work has been done by the Midland Mills Group. The overshot waterwheel has been rebuilt with new buckets and is capable of operating. All the gearing and grindstones are *in situ*, but require new gear teeth and partial rebuilding of the hubs. Unfortunately, recent flooding in July 2007 seriously damaged the weir and washed away sections of the river bank, so it is currently not possible to raise a head of water to pass over the waterwheel.

## The village mill

Aldington was no different from hundreds of other villages and hamlets in the Middle Ages in that it was surrounded by arable land, primitively farmed by the local people. Unfenced common fields were divided into strips and split amongst the village families who grew and harvested corn for bread production.

Originally each household would have had a quern or hand mill, but as technology improved, watermills were developed, aided to some extent by clock making science which employed similar reduction gearing techniques.

Considerable resources in materials and expertise were required for the construction of a village watermill. In most cases this was undertaken by the lord of the manor, and to ensure the venture was a success, all households were required to take their corn to the communal mill.

Initially this was very unpopular and in some instances the personal milling equipment was confiscated or destroyed to enforce the rules.

The choice of wind or water mill was largely decided by the topography of the area and, in the case of watermills, the availability of a reliable water source.

Water sources were indeed a major consideration in the positioning of settlements in the first place. Mankind needed water for his own consumption and his animals, irrigation of the land, and latterly, to drive machinery. Because the methods of transportation of grain were primitive, expensive and time consuming, mills appeared in large numbers throughout the land. Even at the time of the Domesday book in 1086, 271 mills were recorded in Gloucestershire alone.

Generally speaking, watermills were more common than windmills. A stream or river was a more reliable source of power than wind. In some parts of the country this was not true. In East Anglia and Kent, for example, there was usually wind of some strength and the rivers and streams were slow flowing and meandering.

Watermills needed to be carefully sited. A position on a mountain side, or where plenty of drop or fall of water could be achieved, presented little problem. However in a relatively flat area such as Aldington, initially, a primitive form of paddle or undershot wheel would have been used. This required little fall but plenty of flow. The water simply pushed against the wheel paddles as it flowed underneath.

However as man strove to improve the efficiency of waterwheels, more fall was required. By far the most common method of achieving this was, either to create a pond of water upstream of the mill, or to build a leat or channel to carry water alongside the river up to an elevated position in relation to the mill. These leats could be up to a mile long in order to achieve a few feet of water fall at the mill site.

Long leats required considerable upkeep, rather like a canal, to prevent leakage. Also a gate or sluice was fitted at the beginning of the leat which could divert the water into the stream when it was not needed, necessitating a long walk for the miller at the end of the day.

The last mill at Aldington was fed from a pond and employed a sophisticated waterwheel as will be described later in this chapter.

## History

A watermill at Aldington was mentioned in the Domesday book in 1086. The history of the village goes back further: in 703 Offa, King of the East Angles, included Aldington (*Aldingtone* meaning Aelda's town) among the local lands which were presented to the monastery at Evesham. At this time payments of 90 eggs were made annually to the almoner of the monastery to relieve the infirm, the afflicted and the poor.

During his reign at Evesham (1214-1229) Abbot Randolph bought Aldington mill and also built a grange there. Abbot Roger Zatton (1380-1418) replaced this with a 'great grange'. The mill would presumably be supplying flour for this establishment.

By 1300 Aldington had been joined with Badsey which lies a mile to the south east and also had buildings owned by Evesham monastery.

In 1535 the annual value of Aldington and Badsey was £38 5s 4d and they rendered to the monastery 18 quarters of wheat, 26 of barley and 10 of peas and beans (one quarter equals 64 gallons).

In 1539 the mill was leased by the abbot to Thomas and Elizabeth Budgen for the annual rent of 30s 4d. At this time Aldington was commanding a higher rent than Badsey which was then 24 s.

At the dissolution, in 1540 the wealth of Evesham Abbey was broken up and the tenancy of the manor and mill at Aldington was granted to

Richard Pygyon.

In 1562 Queen Elizabeth granted Aldington and Badsey manors to Sir Robert Throckmorton; the Pygyons were still in residence at the mill. Aldington manor changed hands several times in the following years and the mill may sometimes have been part of the package[2]. For example, in 1653 there is an agreement to lease the manor and mill for 21 years.

By 1807 no watermill existed in Aldington and the new owner of the manor, James Ashwin, had a new watermill built on a plot of land adjacent to Manor Farm . The mill was completed by 1814 as deeds relating to a house in Village Street refer to the land attached being bounded by the mill pond to the east.

The ownership of the mill site was transferred to Mr Peter Marriott about 1960. He used the site for various purposes associated with commercial vehicle conversions and scrapping. On his death on 4th February 2005 the ownership passed to his daughter Glynda who still occupies the mill house.

## Location

It is likely that there is more than one place in Aldington where watermills have stood.

There is evidence that the original medieval watermill was located downstream of the village of Aldington, about half a mile to the north of the present site, although it has not been possible to find the exact position. In trying to locate it, the following have been considered:

The confluence of the brooks occurs approx ¼ mile north of the village and the increased water flow of the two streams would certainly have helped to turn an inefficient undershot wheel.

In 1905, at a point below the confluence, according to a period map, the streams appear to split again and rejoin across a field, possibly indicating a mill and bypass. However, this may have been a flood alleviation scheme in an area prone to flooding, or may just have been a large ditch. This is in a field which was used as a football pitch in the late 19th and early 20th century and these features were probably removed in an attempt to achieve a flat pitch.

On the 1883 Ordnance Survey map a large stone building called Sheepditch Barn is shown on the northern bank of the stream. This could have been built from the stone of the original

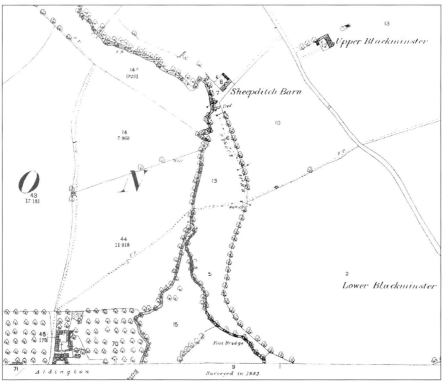

*Extract from the 1883 OS map showing the confluence of the two streams running bottom to top and the location of Sheepditch Barn. It is considered this is very close to the original mill site. Chapel Lane, Aldington is in the bottom left corner of this map.*

mill as it was common practice to reuse materials. Nothing remains today.

On sketches attached to land sales around 1825, the two water meadows in the vicinity are described as Flood Gate Meadow and Mill Ham Meadow.

It cannot be determined when the mill site was moved to its last position adjacent to the Manor Farm. It is possible this happened in the Middle Ages, and it is also possible several mills were built and rebuilt over the centuries. There was no mill shown on the Enclosure Act map of 1807 at that site, but the landowner James Ashwin had one built shortly after that date.

## The buildings and business

The watermill on the present site was built between 1808 and 1814. It was of brick construction and was initially a corn grinding mill. The nearest mill was at Badsey which although it was still grinding corn at that time, was converted to silk throwing by 1818. After that Aldington had a larger catchment area.

A millpond had been created by banking up the brook to raise water height. This had achieved a vertical drop for the water of 8 or 9 feet which meant a low breastshot wheel could be employed. The headrace or water entry passed down the side of the mill building, through the wheel and out through an underground tail race culvert across the mill site to discharge back in to the brook by the ford at the bottom of Mill Lane. Sluice gates controlled the water level on the pond, excess water running round the east side of the site.

A fragment of a cast iron water wheel shroud has been found on the site from which it can be established the wheel was 21 feet in diameter with cast iron shrouds (sides) and 64 wooden buckets. Its width is unknown, but was probably between four and six feet. This should have provided enough power to drive at least two sets of mill stones.

Assuming the quantity of water flowing was similar to today, continuous milling could be achieved. It was not necessary to stop milling periodically to let the level in the pond recover.

The mill would have been of three storey construction. The ground or bottom floor housed the waterwheel, pitwheel and vertical gearing. The

*Above: The recovered cast iron section of the waterwheel showing the integral flanges for the wooden buckets. The diameter was 21 feet.*
*Below: A sketch of how the complete wheel might have looked with shaded section showing the rescued fragment.*

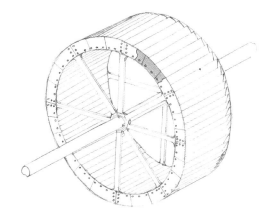

first floor carried the grind stones and grading equipment. The second floor was the grain store with sack hoist and grain shoots down to the stones.

The miller would have operated the mill from the ground floor. Flour would have exited the grind stones on the first floor into a wooden housing or tun from where it passed down shutes to the ground floor where it was bagged.

A lot of flour mills could be operated by one man through a set of ingenious levers and rods. He had complete control over the tentering (the gap between the two grind stones) and consequently the fineness of the flour, the flow of water and therefore the speed of the waterwheel and machinery, and even raise the sacks of grain through a water powered sack hoist. Ancillary equipment driven by belts from the main shafts could include graders, grindstones, bellows for hearths and all form of drills, augers, shears, guillotines and hammers.

The grindstones themselves, of which there were, until recently, several examples scattered around the mill site, would have consisted of a stationery bed or bottom stone with a central hole through which a vertical shaft passed to support and rotate the upper or runner stone. This stone had a central access hole through which the grain entered the space between the two stones.

The speed at which the grain entered and the distance between the two stones was very critical and too much grain would clog the grooves in the face of the stones and overheat.

Millstones, although made of very hard stone, did wear down and required dressing periodically. This task was very often done by travelling stone dressers who called regularly. It is said that the first time a dresser came to a mill the miller would ask him to 'show his metal' or look at his hands to see how many minute particles were embedded in the skin as a way of judging his experience of a very skilled job.

There was accommodation attached to the mill building. This is visible on the only known photograph of the mill taken in the early 1900s and sold as a postcard (reproduced at the start of this chapter). There is a second chimney on the building indicating, in addition to a domestic fire, there could have been a baking oven for bread production.

In the photograph there is another building on the west side of the mill with a large chimney stack. This would have housed a steam engine and Cornish boiler. Ultimately an oil engine was added. These other forms of power generation would have added greatly to the reliability, capacity and capabilities of the mill and were common additions as engine technology improved, very often to the exclusion of the original water power altogether.

The steam engine was certainly installed by 1872 when a valuation figure of £2550 was given for a "substantially built flour and grist mill which has, in addition to a plentiful supply of water, a Cornish boiler and steam engine of 15 horsepower and machinery embracing every modern appliance".

At that time the total area of the mill site, orchard and Lower Mill Meadow was quoted as just over 5 acres. In the local trade directories, Aldington Mills are described as water, steam and oil.

Looking again at the photograph, the mill house, built in the time of miller Jerry Sharp, is in the background, and a number of store buildings on the right. The millpond is in the foreground.

It was fairly common for a drive from the waterwheel to be taken to adjacent buildings, and it seems certain this was the case at Aldington. Not far from the mill building stood a large and imposing three bay barn which remains today. A rotating shaft was run from the mill to this barn (a distance of 30 to 40 feet) where it could have driven a threshing machine or other farm equipment. The shaft which is now under ground level, was exposed recently when a mechanical digger, which was excavating a driveway next to the barn, hooked its bucket under the shaft and bent it upwards slightly.

Millers were often looked upon with suspicion and jealousy by the farmers. It was difficult for the farmers to know how much flour the miller had actually ground. Sometimes the grain was delivered

*A sketch of the mill site showing the layout of the various buildings and the stream.*

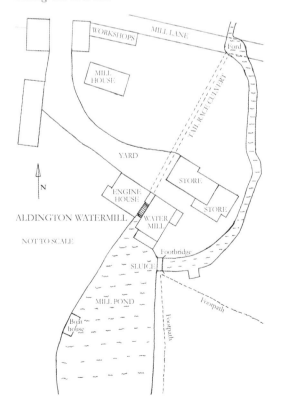

to the miller, ground and the flour returned to the farmer with no money changing hands. The miller simply retained a percentage of the flour for himself.

However, this does not seem to have been the case during Jerry Sharp's time. His accounts book for the period 1885 to 1895 has been saved and gives a fascinating insight into how the mill operated. The entries on the left hand page were the payments made to farmers for grain, calculated by weight. The right hand figures were income.

During the ten years from 1885 (when he took over the mill) until 1896, his annual cash banked rose from £1053 to £2602, which was a considerable sum 110 years ago.

It seems likely that a wide range of engineering work was undertaken at the mill in addition to corn milling. This would have been of greater and greater importance as the 20th century unfolded. Large steam and electric roller mills were being developed which could produce great quantities of high quality flour very quickly.

The small country mills were forced to concentrate on low grade products such as animal feed. Many changed to pulping, board production, crushing and, in fact, anything that could be produced without major investment.

Other factors that affected the demise of the mill were the general state of the agricultural industry at the end of the 19th century, and locally the change from farming to market gardening. Tenant farmer Arthur Savory at Aldington Manor, for example, had been growing 100 acres of wheat each year but this dwindled by 90% and most of that was used for feeding the livestock.

The death in 1916 of Jerry Sharp seems to have started the decline of the mill. It must have remained unused and deteriorating for several years but was demolished shortly before the Marshall family took over in 1938.

The agricultural buildings, workshops and mill house remained. The wheel pit was left open for

*An aerial view of the mill site taken in 1964 in Peter Marriott's time. The loading ramp can be seen in the yard adjacent to the left hand end of the millpond which was the position of the original mill building. A number of vehicles can be seen in the yard. These were coloured maroon and cream and were ex Midland Railway lorries for dismantling or conversion.*

*A page from the miller's accounts book of 1895*

some years after the demolition, and some villagers can remember playing in the pit in the 1950s. Eventually everything was concreted over and a raised loading bay constructed so that trucks could reverse up to it for loading.

Large metal framed storage buildings were erected to the east of the mill site which remain today. These were built to house paper sacks of fertilizer in Peter Marriott's time, but were never used much for that purpose. The sale of fertilizer in plastic bags which could be stored outside was just being introduced, and more importantly, sold direct to customers for storage at their premises.

The outfall from the mill race culvert can still be seen today, by the footbridge at the bottom of Mill Lane. Some water still trickles out of the brick lined structure.

The pond remains to this day although it is badly silted up and no doubt contains all manner of detritus, possibly parts of the original mill! The pond was last dredged in the early 1970s. This was in response to a breaking down of the mill pond sides approximately half way along, from where the stream cut a new course through the meadow and rejoined the main stream just below the sluice gates. The dredged material was used to rebuild the pond banked sides.

The sluice gates remain intact and are of interesting design, being ratchet operated by a metal pole or bar. These are maintaining the level of the pond and will require major attention before long.

### Tenants

The mill built in the early 1800s belonged to the Ashwin family but was occupied by tenants all its life. Prior to the first published census in 1841 the occupiers are unknown, but in that year the Keen family were in place.

Thomas Keen, born in 1797, was the miller and his wife was Lydia They had come from Elmley

Castle, where both Lydia and their son John were born. Another son, Henry, was a baker with a wife Elizabeth and a baby daughter Anne. In 1841 this whole family were living in the accommodation attached to the mill.

By 1851 Thomas and Lydia Keen together with their son Henry and four grandchildren had moved up Main Street in the village to what is now called The White House. Thomas's son John and his family stayed at the mill. As his father was now 64, it is assumed John was doing most of the work. Thomas died in 1854 and Lydia in 1858.

Ten years on, in 1861, with his parents dead, John Keen was living at The White House with just his wife. By 1871 John and Elizabeth had moved to Barn Cottage, Mill Lane in Badsey and he had become a market gardener. There is no recorded miller at Aldington in the 1871 census.

In 1873 a John Blakeman was the miller, and in 1876 one Benjamin Shrimpton and his wife Elizabeth were at the mill. The couple had come from Long Crendon via Preston Bagot and Wolston, Warwickshire and by 1881 were milling back at Wolston. The last record of Benjamin Shrimpton was at Coleshill, Warwickshire where he was listed as a retired miller.

By 1881 Kate Cockbill was living at the mill with her three children. She was described as a 'miller's wife', although this description may be incorrect as there is no evidence that her husband, William Cockbill, was the miller.

However the miller proper, living at The White House, was Thomas Sisam – 'Miller and Baker employing two men'. One of his men was probably Josiah Silver, miller and baker aged 24, being a boarder at Thatch Cottage in Village Street.

Thomas Sisam had hailed from Arrow Mill at Alcester where his father Henry was the miller and from whom Thomas had obviously learnt his trade. He did not stay long and in 1891 aged 50 he was recorded as the manager at Harvington Mill which lay on the River Avon.

In 1885 the business was taken over by Jerry Sharp. His father was Joseph Sharp who had been the miller at Walcot Mill, near Pershore, and by 1861, had moved to Wyre Piddle Mill. Son Jerry had worked with his father until he was 37 when he moved to Aldington with his family, wife Elizabeth and three daughters. More children were born at Aldington, some of whom are buried in Badsey churchyard.

In 1901, an Albert Banning, aged 29, a miller journeyman, his wife Mary and family were living in the cottage at the mill.

Jerry Sharp was probably responsible for the most prosperous period of the mill's life. He had a brick detached house built adjacent to the mill at his own expense which he occupied until his death on 17th February 1916 and which was intended for his son to inherit. In his will he bequeathed all the machinery, plant, implements, tools, horse carts, carriages and other effects used in the business to his son John, together with the option to continue occupation for 20 years after which rent became payable to Ashwin. John also got the hall stand, an iron safe and cupboards from the house. John took over the Mill House and remained there until 1938 when he moved to the Laurels at Offenham.

More importantly for the beneficiaries, son John was given £500 and two houses in Common Road, Evesham; daughter Elizabeth got Faulk Mill House and other buildings and land at Offenham. Daughter Edith got £200 plus dwelling houses and gardens adjacent to Faulk Mill House, and daughter Annie Dora got £800 plus two cottages at Honeybourne.

It can be seen that Jerry Sharp was a wealthy man who left £9900 gross on his death and had accumulated considerable property and land. He was buried with his wife in Badsey churchyard. Although son John took over after his father's death, it is obvious the business started to decline, no doubt affected by the Great War and changing trends in the industry. By 1928 there was no Aldington miller listed in any Trade Directory.

When John Sharp left in 1938, the Marshall family consisting of James Thomas Blaze Marshall and his wife Beatrice Violet took on the lease. They had nine children: sons Mons, Alan, Ivor, Douglas and Thomas; and daughters Noreen, Ena, Josie and Trixie (Beatrice).

The main mill buildings were demolished by the time the Marshalls arrived, possibly for safety reasons. A lot of local children used to play in the wheel pit and on the machinery. The work is thought to have been carried out by Messrs Wheeler & Mansell who were builders in Evesham, probably subcontracted to Arthur Street.

ALDINGTON MILLS,
Near EVESHAM,
June 1890

Mr Field   Bengeworth
Bought of J. SHARP.
Terms—Monthly Accounts.

To Bill Delivered   £2.18.9
July 28   By Cash   1. 0. 0

No. 283 0   Dec 19 1906
Received of Mr. J Collins

| | Sacks | £ | s. | d. | |
|---|---|---|---|---|---|
| Amount | | | 3 | 8 | For J. SHARP, Aldington Mills. |
| Discount | | | | | |
| Received | | | | | |

Signature,

No. 2965   Aldington Mills.
RECEIVED of Mr. E J Collins
the sum of   Shillings, and   10
Pence, for Corn ground   Nov 13 1906
Signed, J Bird

Invoices and receipts from the mill dated 1906. Note they are headed Aldington Mills.

A horse and cart from the mill carrying grain or flour. The man holding the reins is John Waldron Bird who worked at the mill and whose signature appears on some of the headed receipts.

Son Alan Marshall started a transport and haulage business from the mill site and some of the other sons subsequently joined the business.

During the war years Alan's father Tom held the fort while his son served in the Royal Army Corps of Signals. After demobilisation Alan returned to the business which, by 1951, had moved to Oat Street in Evesham. Nationalisation meant Marshalls became part of British Road Services until the mid 1950s. The company still exists today.

By 1953 all the Marshall children had left the family home . At this time daughter Trixie who had married Peter Marriott and was living at Hinton on the Green, moved back to the Mill House with their daughter Glynda to look after her father. Thomas (Tom) died in November 1959 and Beatrice in March 1951.

Peter Marriott took over the site and operated a reclamation and fabrication business. James Taylor occupied some of the site and built commercial vehicle bodies on to chassis.

Marriott was also in transport with his brother and latterly making trailers, supplying firewood, fertilizer storage and buying and selling commercial vehicles. He purchased the Mill House, the land and workshops from Henry Ashwin around 1960 for £900.

Peter and Trixie Marriott's daughter Glynda was brought up at the mill house and married Robert Beames. They moved into accommodation at the end of the large barn adjacent to the mill site. They had a daughter Tracey.

Peter Marriott died on 4th February 2005 aged 84, his wife Trixie had died in 1993 at the age of 73. Glynda and her husband subsequently took over the mill house. Robert Beames died in May 2008. Glynda's daughter occupies the accommodation at the end of the barn with her son Tom.

Certain barns on the site are occupied by a motor factor company Satchells.

## Today and tomorrow

Today the site of Aldington Mill is used for storage and domestic occupation. There remains a good live water supply past the site which varies little in its flow rate for most of the year.

*Members of the Marshall family at Aldington Mill in the early 1950s. Left to right, are Douglas, Ivor, Ena, Thomas, Alan and Tom with their Austin K8 25 cwt 3 way van.*

With the increased awareness of alternative clean energy sources, watermills in many areas of the country are being examined for their suitability for electricity production by using the power of the water to turn generators.

Modern technology means it is not even necessary to have a large waterwheel as part of the process. Small propeller or cross flow turbines can generate useful amounts of power, and electronic control equipment manages the electricity production and even feeds surplus into the National Grid, which incidentally they are legally obliged to accept.

The Aldington site has an approximately three metre head of water. With a couple of small turbines enough electricity could be produced to power a house provided it was properly managed.

So who knows what the future holds for the Aldington Mill site? Perhaps one day the latent power of the Badsey Brook may once more be harnessed to serve mankind.

*The area around Aldington Mill as it appears today. From the top left, clockwise:*

*A solid top grindstone showing tangential grooves for the escape of flour and central rynd or support.*

*The sluice gates as they are today, with the pond water on the right and the outfall to the left.*

*Workshops on the left of the entrance to the mill yard. A sign states the footpath no longer runs through the yard but passes over the ford bridge at the bottom of Mill Lane.*

*A wooden notice board erected by Peter Marriott stating 'General workshop and forge, bodywork and agricultural trailers', now removed.*

*Premises on the right of the mill yard entrance, once stables and then occupied by Mr James Taylor for building commercial vehicle bodies.*

*A brick built extension of the stone workshops, spreading down the right hand side of Mill Lane and used by the occupants of Mill House for various purposes.*

*The weir on the north side of the pond formed with pile driven interlocking panels with concrete poured behind and between them.*

*These photographs were taken by Mike Lovatt who also drew the mill wheel.*

## Notes

1   For the history of Badsey Mill, see articles written by Maureen Spinks on the Badsey website, www.badsey.net.

2   In 1598 Aldington manor was conveyed by Richard and Margaret Griffin to Philip Bigge. In 1614 it was passed to William Courten and John Mounsey. A friend of William Courten, George Carew, who had lived in Aldington for many years entered into a complicated legal arrangement with William Courten and William Gerrard or Jarrett to lease the manor and mill for 21 years from 1653. Several other indentures followed involving a number of other parties until in 1665 'all that Manor, Aunton Farm as it was now known and all other messuages etc' was sold to the celebrated ironmaster Thomas Foley of Witley, Worcs. The farm was still in the tenure of William Jarrett at that time and remained so after the sale. The Foley family owned the manor for the next 150 years until the 5th Baron Foley of Kidderminster died and the property was sold off in 1806 to several people. The manor was bought by a George Day of Evesham for £7,000, who on the 6th October 1808 sold it to Mr James Ashwin of Bretforton for £12,000. By 1805 no watermill existed in Aldington and the new owner of the manor, James Ashwin had a new watermill built on a plot of land adjacent to Manor Farm. The Ashwin family were landowners and their family had occupied Bretforton Manor since 1540 when they had moved there from the family seat at Honeybourne. There was a continuous line through to 24th May 1760 when the James Ashwin we are concerned with was born. He married Kitty and they had 2 daughters Mary and Ann. Kitty died in 1796 and James married again (Rebecca) and they had eight further children. One of his sons Richard was installed in Aldington manor after his father had bought it. He died in 1866. During the Ashwin family occupation of the manor it was extended considerably. Today this extension is known as The Manor House and the original building is separately occupied and known as Manor Court. The last Ashwin to occupy Bretforton Manor was Henry Ashwin who died in 1983 at the age of 76. He never married.

## Acknowledgments

With grateful thanks to Mick Taylor, Glynda Beames, Josie Grove and committee members of the Badsey Society who provided a lot of the detail in this chapter.

## Midland Mills Group

For further information about research, conservation and restoration of mills contact: The Society for the Protection of Ancient Buildings (SPAB), Windmill and Watermill Section, 37 Spital Square, London E1 6DY. A regional mills group meets regularly in Birmingham. Contact: Midland Mills Group, Membership Secretary, Mr Tony Perryer, Whitcot Mill, Bishops Castle, Shropshire SY9 5EB.

C H Gardiner was deeply interested in the local traditions of the Vale and the Cotswolds. The Mummers Plays fascinated him and he wrote his own version which was broadcast on the BBC Home Service in one episode of 'Upper Slocombe'.

The picture shows a Mummers Play being performed at Christmas 1951. Brian Jennings remembers the occasion: "We performed the Mummers Play that Christmas at several places. I remember in particular the night of Christmas Eve when we performed in the splendid lounge room at Wickhamford Manor for the owners and their Christmas guests – and we were well entertained afterwards. The play was the traditional English Mummers Play with conflict, death and revival and all that symbolises. As far as I remember St George killed the dragon, the Turkish Knight slew St George and the Doctor with his potion brought them back to life again. The picture was taken in the parish room at the old Badsey Vicarage which was all demolished years ago. The Doctor I think was Ralph Taylor, Derek Barrand was St George, Austen Jones (market gardener of Badsey Fields Lane) was the Moroccan Prince, John Major (a maths teacher at Prince Henry's Grammar School) was Father Christmas and I was the Turkish Knight." An entry in the parish magazine tells us the cast also included A L Byrd, B F P Blake and R Salter.

PHOTO: EVESHAM JOURNAL

# 7

## CHARLES HENRY GARDINER

JANE NEILL

C H Gardiner.

It all began with a slim volume, in a faded dust cover, I found sitting on the bookshelf in my mother's old farmhouse attic. I pulled it off the shelf and read the title *Your Village and Mine*[1] by C H Gardiner. I took it home to read and was enchanted by the down-to-earth common sense and humour describing the life and times of villages, in the Cotswolds and the Vale of Evesham. Written in 1943, in the middle of World War II, it provides a fascinating picture of a changing rural way of life. It was only when I was talking about my find with local friends that I discovered Gardiner once lived in my own small village of Aldington. My curiosity about his life has led me on a fascinating journey. I would like to share his story with you.

Charles Henry Gardiner was born in 1902 at Rodborough in Gloucestershire. His father was a journeyman tailor and his mother was a cook. He was educated at Cirencester Grammar School, where he obtained his senior school certificate with honours. Shortly after leaving school he entered the office of local solicitor H St G Rawlins where he quickly gained experience with the Cirencester Board of Guardians and the Cirencester Rural District Council to which he was officially appointed assistant clerk in 1923. In 1924 he obtained first prize in the final examination of the Institute of Poor Law Accountants. Charles married Miriam Ewart in Bristol in 1925. Their only child, a daughter, Mimosa Miriam, was born in the same year[2].

Charles Gardiner was appointed Clerk to both the Pebworth and Evesham Rural District Councils in 1928, at the early age of 26. First he lived in Bretforton with his young family. Dolly Plant, who lived in that village as a girl, remembers that he wrote plays for the local primary school. In the late 1930s he moved to Ivy House in

Aldington which he made his home until about 1957. He made his final move into one of two Aldington houses built by the Council on orchard land previously belonging to the Byrd family. His house was named *Green Bank*. The other house was occupied by Dr Murray, the Medical Officer of Health. Charles Gardiner and Dr Murray were among the few people to have cars in the village at that time.

Mick Taylor, who was brought up in Aldington, remembers Gardiner as a short, stocky man. He was 'a true gentleman' according to Arthur Plant who lived opposite him for some years.

Charles Gardiner's duties as Clerk to the RDC were manifold. Much of his long working life was spent in the villages around Evesham in Worcestershire. He was particularly suited to this task as he knew village life and understood the co-existing intricacies of a rural economy and community. He wrote a treatise called *'Order Gentlemen, Please' A Guide to Meetings*. In this he set out to explain, as simply as possible, all the rules for conducting a well ordered meeting. "As one who attends close on 400 meetings a year in various capacities of Clerk, Secretary, Chairman and Committee member, I have often thought what a saving of time (and temper) would result if everyone present was thoroughly acquainted with the rules of meetings and resolved to abide by them."

In *Your Village and Mine* he charts the history of the village from its beginnings in a mainly agrarian society to the present (1943) encompassing the gradual changes through the centuries: the medieval open field system, enclosures begun in the reign of Elizabeth I, the agricultural revolution and the large estates, the rising poverty, crime and beggary of the 18th century. In the 19th century, machinery was being introduced into the country as well as the towns, bringing disorder with machine smashing by the poor labourers whose wages were reduced in 1834. Any dissent or assemblies of workers were threatened with transportation to Australia for seven years. The Tolpuddle Martyrs, who dared to form a 'Society' is a famous example of the harshness of the times. They were transported but were returned after a public outcry. Gardiner explains the development of Rural Government, the 1834 Poor Law Unions that set up workhouses,

removing the obligation on every village for maintaining its own poor, the Board of Guardians and the 1870 Education Act which provided education for all children. In 1888 County Councils were formed and in 1894 the Rural District Councils were set up. He writes: "1894 also saw the advent of the Parish Councils in the place of the old vestry meetings. This village parliament was endowed with much wider powers than the average townsman realises. Unfortunately far too many parish councils have failed to exercise fully the powers granted them."

Gardiner ends the chapter with the rise of the motor car after the Great War, weekend cottages and the drift from the land. He concludes: "Village history makes unhappy reading; but it is not without its bright spots as we shall see when we survey the village of today."

Looking from the 1943 perspective, Gardiner discusses the village institutions: the church, the manor and the inn; "and the cynics say that the inn is the only one likely to survive." In discussing the

*Gardiner's homes in Aldington.*
*Opposite: Two photos of Ivy House that once stood at the corner of Mill Lane and Chapel Lane in Aldington. The house was demolished about 1970 and the land sold for The Hop Gardens development. Ivy Cottages were allowed to remain and can just be seen in the lower picture looking along Chapel Lane. The photos were kindly lent by Michael Barnard whose grandfather lived in Ivy House.*
*Below: Green Bank was built by Evesham Rural District Council about 1957 for council employees.*

PHOTO: ROBIN NEILL

church, he does not forget the important role of the chapel. He suggests that "there is no reason why each religious body should not respect the others and combine in movements to aid the common weal, and to right the many wrongs prevailing in this war-ridden world." Gardiner emphasises the role of the manor but the village is dependent on the good will of the squire. He tells amusing anecdotes of pompous squires but many more of the genuinely kind and generous ones. He regrets how the last war and the present conflict have seen the end of some family lines and many have not been able to carry on the family traditions of the country estates. Of the inn, he sees it as a place for the local labourers to have their bread and cheese and a pint of beer or cider, a forum of local and political discussion and entertainment with traditional games. CHG goes on to say: "In wartime many inns have been temporarily ruined from a local and social angle by the influx of workmen engaged on government contracts and earning high wages. The shortage of beer and considerably reduced opening hours have had a bad effect on those places where the population was greatly increased."

Charles Gardiner was a great advocate of the Women's Institute as he often gave talks and observed them at work. He noticed that the members' knowledge of the rules of debate and procedures at meetings was equal if not superior to that of many local authorities. However he felt the formal business could well be relieved by "the occasional introduction of a little humour".

In his book, Charles describes the attributes needed for his role as Clerk to the Council thus, "The Clerk to the Council should regard himself as Public Relations Officer, keeping himself well informed as to local opinion by moving about among the people of the district and maintaining liaison with the press. Close contact with parish councils and attendance at their meetings produces valuable results and removes misunderstandings. Above all, the Clerk should be informal and approachable ... everything in country districts is run on a personal basis ... a sense of humour is an indispensable asset."

## Roads and road men

Charles Gardiner keeps the old ways alive with his literary skills, recording a lost world that's now just a memory. One such is the Cotswold roads. "The native stone roads were as much part of the Cotswolds scene as the stone walls, churches and barns. Many a steep lane winding up the hillside like a golden snake was a landmark visible for miles and the honest country smell of limestone after rain is something I cannot describe but which I always remember." He goes on to describe how the quality of roads depends on the stones used from each quarry. This use was best left to a knowledgeable foreman born and bred in the district. "With the passing of the Cotswold stone road went the rural stone breaker, who was a familiar figure on country lanes before the First World War, as he rode to work very early each morning on his tricycle 'to crack 'em and whack 'em for 9d a day'. " He says that such men are hard to find nowadays but if you know when and where to look for him, the old fashioned stone breaker can still be found: "All that John carries with him on his long walk from the valley is his hammer, his dinner and a little tin. The tin is important, for it contains the grease to prevent the wooden shaft of the hammer from chafing his fingers and palms." Most stone breakers were considered honest men, their work paid piece work above the agricultural wage. It was difficult to find young men to do it as it was still associated with prison and workhouse labour – long since discontinued.

In *Your Village and Mine* CHG tells us about the local road man, Bill 'Willum' Jones, "a character if ever there was one. He belongs to a bygone generation and to see him sitting at the roadside with a clay pipe stuck to his cap and a red handkerchief laid on his knees while eating his lunch, never fails to give me pleasure." Terry Sparrow of Badsey remembers Bill (or Cungar) had a little barrow with a bar on it to hook onto the back of his bike.

Gardiner records in his article *Unconscious Humour* the following sayings of an old road man remembered by an octogenarian from Shipston-on-Stour:

"All my best taters be bad."

"Yur! Put this bit o' string in your pocket, then you'll have some when you've got none."

"I tied my hoss to a gap in the hedge and when I went back thear he were gone."

## Mummers plays

Charles Gardiner recorded the history of the Mummers plays: "In those few villages where it is still performed the mummers play is a survival from the days when country folk were compelled to provide their own entertainment in simple ways. This play, which is associated with the Christmas festivities, later adapted for Plough Monday or Easter, comes in the same category as the folk song handed down by word of mouth. Rarely did farmers or better off country folk take part, moreover, few married men – usually boys or young men." (See the illustration at the beginning of this chapter.)

The plays probably originated from the 15th century as pure comedy although they start with a murder. This varies from village to village. Gardiner looked at over 30 of the plays collected by Reginald Tiddy, an Oxford scholar killed in action in 1916. Tiddy's manuscript was published by friends in 1923: *The Mummers Play*, Oxford University Press. But for this, they may have been lost forever. Briefly, the play was about the killing of St George or the King in combat by a foreign adversary and tells how life was restored by a doctor or medicine man who administers some magic potion after extracting an enormous tooth from the prostrate victim. Father Christmas acts as a master of ceremonies on the stage throughout. In some versions faces were blacked and it was performed at the manor house, inn and cottages. Gardiner wrote a radio version for *Upper Slocombe* which was broadcast on the Home Service.

## Returning Officer and other offices

One of Charles Gardiner's many duties as the clerk to the RDC was as Returning Officer for elections across the county. On May 27th 1952, he gave a 15 minute evening radio broadcast on this subject at the Birmingham studios for the Midland Home Service. It was a demanding task with elections taking place in over 30 rural districts and 20 or more parish councils with between 5 and 13 members on each council. With several hundred candidates there was a need for "scrupulous fairness and impartiality ... Counting votes in this kind of election is a dreary business. There is no short cut."

The greatest change he cited was the vote for women over 21 in 1928. At first, the women came with a male escort. The Women's Institute and other women's organisatic... the female villagers making them more cc... Another change, for ti... of a show of hands in p...

"The present day villa... it's not many years ago th... opposing such projects as l... supplies, sewerage schemes a... , solely on the ground that such pro... would increase rates."

As always, Gardiner had many amusing and interesting experiences to recount. Not every vote counted, as one ballot paper he received had the following rhyme written on the back:

> Thompson isn't old enough
> I don't care for Mr Gough
> Nor do I care for Mr Dare
> I've spoilt my vote I do declare!

"While there was no laxity ... for many a presiding officer it is a social occasion. In a village at the foot of the Cotswolds an elderly widow entered the polling station. She had a sharp way of speaking and was suspicious of what she regarded as excessive civility on the part of the presiding officer when he said 'Good afternoon, madam', for in the village she was usually addressed as 'Missus' or 'Mother'. She looked at him and snapped, 'Don't you madam me, young man. A madam's a French 'ooman, and I be British to the backbone!'"

It was a secret vote but an officer could not stop someone declaring his choice as he deposited his ballot paper in the box – or ensuring that there was no pressure to vote for a particular candidate. CHG tells the tale of a doctor who used subtle tactics to secure votes. The doctor rarely charged his patients but at election time he would drop into the conversation with the villagers that it was time accounts were settled. "Time and again he was elected. He would ask friends over to the surgery to celebrate victory – taking glasses from the cupboard and dragging a case of beer from the corner – he took two large blue bottles marked 'Poison' off the shelf assuring them it was whisky and gin. Although the doctor sampled with relish the poison from his bottle, this was an occasion when confirmed spirit drinkers amongst the

company hearti... best!"... Putti... stre...

subscribed to the slogan 'Beer is

...ing up a poster giving instructions was not ...ghtforward either. Using the names Smith, Jones and Brown as examples was not without its dangers as these names inevitably came up on ballot papers. One ingenious official got round the problem by substituting Alpha, Beta and Gamma. "Soon after this change," Mr Gardiner writes, "I saw two aged villagers standing in the same voting compartment, looking puzzled – I went across and asked 'Is there anything you don't understand?' I pointed to Messers Alpha, Beta and company and one asked, 'Who be these three varmints?' Then he added firmly, 'We don't want nern o' they there furriners up yur'."

Occupations of a candidate raised a few eyebrows with Mr Gardiner too. "Farmer must be the most elastic occupation in the English countryside used by a business magnate, squire and smallholder alike." Also he remembers someone wrote "Age 30. Height 5 feet 11 inches. Eyes brown. Dark complexion!"

Gardiner concluded that "being a Returning Officer may have its worries and responsibilities, but if the man who holds it has a sense of humour, it can never be dull."

Lionel Knight, a colleague of Gardiner for many years, remembers that the officials always collected at the pub afterwards. He remembers Charlie's "One for the road" became legendary.

Mr Gardiner's other duties included being the Superintendent Registrar of Births, Marriages and Deaths. He married many of the locals at the Register Office and kept in touch with many of those local couples he married. He was greatly suited for such a position where his discretion and sympathy for every human condition were invaluable. On one occasion, according to his obituary in the *Evesham Standard*, "he was urgently telephoned by a cleric, who, suspecting that a bridegroom already at the altar was about to commit bigamy, had locked the surprised man in the vestry while Mr Gardiner's wisdom could be consulted. 'Tell him to apologise and go away quietly and never see the girl again' was the advice." CHG was a very sociable and approachable man and was greatly respected in the community.

Among his many tasks, he was clerk to the Board of Guardians, the South Worcestershire Assessment Committee, the Joint Water Committee, the Joint Fire Brigade Committee, the Joint Ambulance committee and many other bodies. His obituary says, "Yet, with all that multiplicity of official posts, he was devoid of all pomp and had no feeling whatever of his own importance. He was never a bureaucrat, always a human being with a warm-hearted courtesy and an irresistible sense of humour. In one capacity he would write severe letters to himself in another, and then send disarming replies." Gardiner was to describe his function as being that of a rural Poo-Bah.

## World War II

During World War II, Mr Gardiner became Food Officer, Chief Reception Officer for Billeting, and Clerk of the War Agricultural Executive Committee. In the BBC Archives, there is a recording of Mr Gardiner talking, in 1948, about his role billeting evacuees called *How do you spell 'Yokels'?*

"Looking back at all the difficulties it's clear, for the most part, this great social upheaval was met successfully and with good will but there were bound to be exceptions. Children were received into homes totally different from those they had left in the cities. Thus, one foster mother found two children sleeping under the bed in which they'd been placed earlier in the evening. Some had no idea how to use cutlery beyond a spoon, others had never previously tasted certain fresh vegetables, while there were demands for fish and chips in place of the well cooked country meals. Some children were dirty but not many. In most cases the services rendered by the foster parents went far beyond the very modest allowance which was 10/6d a week, for one child, and 8/6d a week where more than one was taken. They bought the children clothes, gave them pocket money, toys and even bicycles. Among the thousands billeted, I came across no case of physical cruelty and we would certainly have heard about it for, although, it's said "one half of the world doesn't know how the other half lives", that doesn't happen in the English village. My first experience of evacuated children in my own house was amusing. Three girls were sent to us. After a wash and a meal my wife gave them note paper and envelopes and suggested that they write a letter to their parents telling them of their whereabouts and safe arrival. The children scribbled industrially for a minute or two, then one looked up and asked "How do you spell 'yokels'?" So much for the clerk of the council and his family!"

His job as Clerk to the RDC would be demanding enough for any man but Mr Gardiner combined this with his literary career in his spare time. He compiled a small book, published by the *Evesham Standard*, called *Future of Evesham and District – A Survey of Factors Affecting Post-War Reconstruction and Development*. The preface, written by the editor of the *Evesham Standard*, said "Mr Gardiner, whose deep interest in, and intimate knowledge of conditions in the Vale, is widely acknowledged, responded ... with a comprehensive and authoritative survey which aroused wide interest when it appeared in the Standard". The book covers the history of the market garden movement which, CHG says, started in Badsey in 1865. He explains the unique Evesham Custom, the handing on of the tenancy to the next generation of market gardeners formally recognised on the Rudge Estate in 1872. "It is significant that the Evesham RDC continued to lend money throughout the depression to small market gardeners wishing to purchase or build houses of their own."

When considering housing provision, Gardiner contrasted the population growth in market gardening areas like Badsey with traditional agricultural villages such as Pebworth. In Badsey, in 1841, the census shows a population of 395 increasing to 1,189 in 1931; whereas Pebworth had a population of 828 in 1841 declining to 558 in 1931. For the rural district, which comprised 28 villages, Gardiner proposed that 150 houses needed to be built in the first year after the war but putting that into practise was more problematic as building materials and labour were in short supply. The RDC had the advantage over the Evesham Town Council in that they owned their own land.[4]

He maintained "The most pleasing aspect of the activities of existing rural community councils is the friendly and informal way in which they work. Such is the only one likely to be successful in rural affairs in which everything is conducted on a personal and not a bureaucratic basis".

He expressed the view that "the value of a technical education and scientific research is becoming widely appreciated." He found it "strange that such an important agricultural and horticultural area as the Vale of Evesham had no technical centre for agricultural education, discussion or research". A university college offering such an opportunity was needed.

## Joseph Arch

Charles Gardiner wrote a piece called *Country Crusade: The Life and Times of Joseph Arch (1826-1919)* coauthored with John H Bird[5] who was the Evesham Journal's staff man at Stratford -upon-Avon. They wrote:

"Joseph Arch devoted himself with all his rustic vigour to the task of securing fair reward and decent social conditions for all who worked on the land." The article describes the amazing rise of this poor Warwickshire labourer who left school at nine to carry on his letters at his mother's kitchen table. Against all the odds he was the first labourer to become an MP and the first to become a county councillor. He campaigned for the formation of the parish councils and set up the Smallholdings Act. He advocated legislation for giving security of tenure. Arch founded the Agricultural Labourers Union. "He realised that only Parliament could give back to the labourers the land taken from them under the enclosures. Accordingly he fought for votes for the rural workers in order that they might have means to influence Parliament towards meeting their aspirations."

Agricultural labourers, at that time, had no voting rights. The enclosures had robbed them of land to subsidise their meagre, seasonal livings and they lived in abject poverty having to rely on the workhouse for charity to get them through the winter months. But the authors noted that there were exceptions: "It is certain, however, that the happy conditions prevailing on Mr Savory's farm were exceptional".[3]

Gardiner and Bird recorded meeting a Mrs Fairfax and other people who had known Joseph Arch. They regaled tales of the great man who remained loyal to his roots and his upbringing, ending his days quietly in his birthplace.

## Cider making

Mr Gardiner recorded the tradition of cider making in the Vale of Evesham in an article written while living at Ivy House in Aldington. He tells "A stone's throw from my house in a village in the Vale of Evesham stands a barn-like building constructed in the typical half-timbered Worcestershire style. During the greatest part of the year it stands neglected but in the autumn it's the centre of activity with much coming and going, for it's a cider mill – And here and now I'd like to dispel the impression that cider has been rationalised on a business basis and is no longer a local brew."

He goes on to describe the cider mill both past and present. "Cider mill, now, is a misnomer as most have been dismantled. It was a circular stone trough about 19 inches wide and 15 inches deep with the overall diameter of about 10 feet. This continuous round is called 'the chase'. Fixed to an arm stretching out from a central pillar is a huge circular grindstone weighing the best part of a ton and held in a upright position. It rotates slowly round the chase when drawn by an old horse harnessed to a projecting arm. The apples are tipped into the chase and crushed into pulp by the heavy grindstone. The pulp or *pummy* is then removed and placed between hair-cloths sandwich fashion, one piled upon another, in a stack beneath a powerful press. The stack is called a 'cheese' and the press is turned by a wooden lever on the capstan principle with slow but tremendous pressure until the juice runs out from the pulp and is collected in a open vat below. From here, the fresh apple juice is baled out into large barrels which are taken away to the farm or cottage where the liquid is transferred to large casks formerly containing wines and spirits. It is allowed to ferment and finally the bung is closed."

But by Gardiner's time the technology had changed. "Now the fruit is crushed by a mechanical 'scratter' or 'scratcher' worked by a pulley driven by a portable engine. The fruit and the large open barrels were once carried by horse and dray – a common sight – now it is a lorry or trailer. Ours is essentially a communal mill. Each villager who wants to make cider brings his own fruit to the mill and he's expected to find his own labour. Among the workmen and smallholders this labour is usually provided on the basis of reciprocal services. Good neighbours help one another in turn, as often happens in a rural community. But superintending it all is a general factotum who is in continuous attendance at the mill throughout the cider making season. This presiding genius is invariably a well-known local character who can stand a joke and whose repartee is of a high order."

"Last year we had Vicky who cycled from the next village – to him and his kind cider- making is a labour of love ... Vicky's tribute consists of ample quantities of the best of last years cider. Old Frankie (now dead and gone) who supervised the mill in a neighbouring village went one better than Vicky. He demanded 3 star brandy – and got it! Not like sweet bottled cider, it's called "rough", "local" or "hedgerow" cider in the Vale of Evesham and "scrumpy" on the Cotswolds. But it can be very potent, especially when in prewar days a knowledgeable countryman decided to "feed" a barrel (to use a local expression) by inserting beef-steak, honey and other secret agents."

"These had the effect of increasing alcohol content and clearing the liquid of the cloudiness observed in ordinary rough cider."

"Even untreated cider sometimes turns out to be strong, especially if it has been kept in a freshly emptied barrel, which previously contained spirits. I call to mind what happened, some years ago, when an innkeeper came across a barrel of cider that had been overlooked and without first sampling it, put it on tap. It immediately roused the fighting propensities of his customers ... A poor hen-pecked little man with a wife like an Amazon went home and turned over the supper table. She was so astonished that she burst into tears. This potent brew was hurriedly withdrawn from circulation."

"There were vintage years for cider, too, for in a warm friendly summer the apples hoard the sunshine and release it in the autumn juice. In the Vale of Evesham and indeed in many parts of Britain, cider is the land workers' natural drink. It goes down particularly well at lunchtime under the hedge or in a shed with bread and cheese and an onion. It's comparatively cheap to make and above all, free from tax. In our part of the country, at least, it will be a long time before local cider is supplanted by an alien mass-produced beverage."

**Radio and television**

In 1936 Charles Gardiner wrote a comedy play *Motor Cars or Hosses?* set around 'the deplorable episodes in the history of the Parish Council of the Cotswold village of Upper Slocombe'. *The Radio Times* stated: "One day out of the blue, a script came into the office and it was so good that it simply had to be produced. But there was a snag in it. Many of the parts were in Cotswold dialect. The difficulty was got over by enlisting the services of some amateurs from Worcestershire and with their help the play is to be presented tonight" (March 18th at 7.15 pm).

The play was so successful it led to many more including *Pump and Circumstance*, *The Murder of Anne Cornell*, *The Fatal Step*, *Upper Slocombe Calling*, *The Mummers Play*, *The Vale of Evesham*, *Uncle Hiram's Chair*, *Charity Begins at Upper Slocombe*, *The Champ*, *Country Elections*, *Burnt Norton* and *The Bold Peasantry*. The producers continued to use the authentic voices of genuine local people such as Bob Arnold, Bill Payne, Lionel Ellis, Garnet Keyte, George Hart and John Hall. Charles Gardiner often took part himself.

According to the accounts for the broadcast of *Pump and Circumstance* in 1937, Charles Gardiner was paid fifteen guineas (£15.75) while the actors were paid between four and eight guineas. Lionel Ellis's widow Dorrie remembers that the cast would all retreat to the pub over the road from the Birmingham recording studios for a well-deserved drink. Judith Ellis, Lionel's daughter, remembers the large box of Black Magic chocolates that her father would bring home to her mother at a time when chocolates were a luxury.

Three of the actors went on to take parts in *The Archers* from 1950. George Hart was the original Tom Forrest to be replaced by Bob Arnold a year later. In 1967, George Hart returned to take on the role of Jethro Larkin and Bill Payne was Ned Larkin for many years.

Gardiner was always suggesting new local feature programmes for the Midland Home Service. This is illustrated in a letter he wrote to a producer in 1937. "It occurred to me that 'Blossom Time in the Vale of Evesham' would make a pleasing and interesting feature and I'm enclosing notes about it which I've very hurriedly thumped out with two awkward fingers! If I'm too late or the idea isn't practicable, don't hesitate to say so, because I've not spent many minutes on it. As a further idea, what about a 15 minute feature on asparagus – which is something of a mystery as regards commercial cultivation to many people who eat it? Kind regards..."

The programme went ahead encompassing both the blossom and asparagus under the title of *The*

*The 'Upper Slocombe' team. From left to right: Bill Payne, George Hart, John Hall, Bob Arnold, Lionel Ellis, Garnet Keyte, Bill Hughes and Charles Gardiner. Photograph kindly lent by Dorrie and Judith Ellis of Chipping Campden.*

# MOTOR CARS OR HOSSES?

A truthful account of one of the more deplorable episodes in the history of the Parish Council of the Cotswold Village of Upper Slocombe

# PUMP
## *and*
## CIRCUMSTANCE

A play about troubled waters. The fight that was waged in Upper Slocombe between those who wanted water supply by pipes and...

**7.30 'PUMP AND CIRCUMSTANCE'**

A Faithful Account of another Deplorable Episode

in the History of the Parish Council of the Worcestershire Village of Upper Slocombe

Reconstructed from the Unofficial Records

by C. H. Gardiner

and

Re-enacted by a Group of Local Inhabitants

The Hero...............The Village Pump
The Villain................Jians Gubbins

Produced by Owen Reed

*Vale of Evesham.* It was arranged by Robin Whitworth in co-operation with Gardiner. Rehearsal took place on Saturday April 10th 1937, from 5 to 9 pm and on the following Monday until 5 pm. Transmission time was 8.45 to 9.25 pm that evening. It was scripted by Gardiner using the local people's own words to describe various aspects of the orchard and asparagus cultivation. Frank Clarke on the blossom, C A Binyon and Ralph Smith on asparagus, John Hall on cutting the gras, Walter Harwood (of Long Ashton) on the research stations, Mrs. Byrd, Jack Bent, Adam Howley, Jack Hodges, Mrs. Heritage on various tasks and Jimmy 'Teapot' talking about bird minding in the orchards. Jimmy Teapot's script went like this:

John Hall: Some minders carry a gun, don't they?
Teapot: Yes, but I don't. I don't hold with the
    birds being shot – the only guns I carries is me
    old short pipe and I wouldn't be without that
    'un for summat.
Hall: What about breakfast?
Teapot: Well just a mouthful to keep out the cold.
    2 pounds o' bacon and a small loaf.
Hall: That ought to keep the cold out. What
    about dinner?
Teapot: Two pound of beef and three pounds of
    fried onions done on the devil.
Hall: I suppose you have a bit of supper?
Teapot: Oh, Ah! I has a bit of supper - A nobble
    of cheese about the size of a brick and the
    top of a fower pound loaf and a drop of cider
    with some eggs broke in it.

In 1956, Charles Gardiner was in correspondence with the BBC organising a *Woman's Hour* 10 minute slot of Cotswold songs in collaboration with Bob Arnold (the voice of Tom Forrest for 47 years in

The Archers) a true Cotswolds countryman living in Burford at this time. He wrote the scripts to describe the origin of the songs they had chosen with care so as not to offend the ladies (*The Bellringers* was considered too risqué) and they both performed the singing either on their own or together. Gardiner was asked to attend rehearsals on Christmas Eve 1956. It must have been a success because they were still performing on the June 25th 1958 *Woman's Hour*. On that occasion CHG sang *The Cumberland Drinking Song* with Bob Arnold and *Nothing Else to do* as a solo.

As well as radio he made an appearance on television in Wilfred Pickles' *At Home*. Norman Swallow of the Talks Department of the Television Service sent him the following letter dated November 14th 1950, from Alexandra Palace, Wood Green, N22: "This is just to confirm our arrangements for Saturday, November 18th. First of all, about rehearsal times and how to get to the studios: As Alexandra Palace is some distance from London, we have arranged for you to all to be taken there by the BBC Transport from Broadcasting House, Portland Place (near Oxford Circus) leaving there at 1.15 pm ... my secretary, Miss Judy Letherby, will meet everybody in the entrance hall ... In order that she may be recognised she will carry a pink coloured folder, tied with string ... About dress; our cameras at Alexandra Palace react badly to black, white, spots and stripes! Anything else will do, but it would be extremely kind if you could bring along shoes with rubber soles to save noise ... I am sending you a list of 17 questions Wilfred (Pickles) and I have worked out between us and which we would like people to study before the weekend so that you will know what sort of questions, etc are likely to be sprung on you ...We usually end these programmes by asking everybody in turn to say something, very briefly, about their attitudes to life or something about which they happen to feel very strongly – perhaps you would think up something along these lines so that you won't be caught unawares...". Swallow continued that he had booked a single room for Gardiner at the Mascot Hotel, 6 York Street, London, W1.

## Local dialect

Charles Gardiner was fascinated by the Cotswold and Vale of Evesham dialects[6]. He was eager to preserve as much as he could in writing before it was changed forever with the encroachment of modernity. He was very aware of this danger. He wrote "Nobody can deny that dialect speech on the Cotswolds is declining. Some words that I heard as a boy in the South Cotswolds have disappeared although when a word seems to have gone forever it reappears in conversation with a Cotswold native and not necessarily an old one at that." He was most fascinated by the Campden and Ebrington dialects as very distinct in the North Cotswolds but wrote that "these local differences are most marked in the Vale of Evesham where it is possible to go from one village to another only one mile away to hear a distinctly different speech. There is a good reason for this – in the Vale not only has there been no migration to the towns, but not even from one village to another."

In his journal, Gardiner wrote "Most of my dialect writing has been done for radio and stage plays and for country speakers to broadcast. A mistake that I made in the early days was overdoing the phonetic spelling in scripts for talk, plays and documentary features." He decided with the advice of the BBC Producer he was working with to give an "intelligent Cotswold farm carter" appearing in a feature programme a script in standard English. The carter was told to write it as he'd say it to a friend in the inn. The carter had altered very few words, for example, "frozen" to "frez", "frightened" to "frit" and "something" to "summat". When he came to speak it the carter pronounced "again" as "agyun", "week" as "wick" and so on. Gardiner came to the conclusion that writing in dialect was too cumbersome and trying to read. He kept it to a minimum.

Charles Gardiner collaborated with Hugh Massingham, a well known local writer of the time. Together they wrote *The Country Comedy*. CHG collected and recorded many comic country tales. It was to be the basis for the many articles he published in the *Evesham Journal* later in his career. He wrote "In a class of its own is the humour of the old folk ... the working countrymen and women who have achieved a measure of independence towards the end of a long and hard life. The women in particular display a mordant wit and use it without a smile."

Gardiner tells the story of a widow being visited

by the parson. He enquired about her health and she replied "Very middling" and it would not be long before she rested on "Absolom's bosom". When the vicar remonstrated that she meant Abraham's bosom, she replied that if he'd been a widow as long as she had, he would be glad of anybody's bosom.

Rural characters were his inspiration. Such as Jimmy 'Teapot' Williams, the great eater from Chipping Campden, whom he had the delight of watching devour a huge meal once, and Tommy Boots of Yubberton (Ebrington) whose lying was legendary. These were characters that lived on by reputation. One humorous tale he recorded was also about the Ebrington locals.

Two men meet in the street one carrying a pail.
"Whur be you a-going, Jumps (James)?"
"I b'ent going nowheres" said Jumps.
"Of course you be, with that pail".
"No I b'ent. I be a-coming back".

He always had the greatest respect for the local language and idiosyncrasies recording "Rarely is a countryman inarticulate in his native tongue."

## Jimmy 'Teapot' Williams

Gardiner wrote about and used the voices of real Cotswold characters on the radio. When Jimmy

*Jimmy Teapot scaring the birds in an orchard. Photograph by Ernest Lockyer, used with kind permission of Clive Lockyer.*

'Teapot' Williams from Chipping Campden died on April 14th 1953 aged 77 years, Gardiner wrote *An Appreciation of a Remarkable Character* with Bill Payne. It was transmitted on the Midlands Home Service on 18th November 1953. Gardiner tells us how Jimmy Teapot was often asked how he came by this unusual nickname. He thought it was an uncle who gave it to him and when the uncle died the name stuck. He seemed to like this name for he used to say: "I be the one and only Teapot except him that stands on the hob". He had a withered leg from childhood paralysis and always carried a stick. He was called for medical examinations several times during World War I and the service doctor once remarked "Williams, you're the fittest man I've ever examined – above the knees!" The late Hugh Massingham described him as "a living myth". His eating capacity was indeed a legend. He describes a prewar supper in the pub – a pint of cider – " With this he would consume a very large piece of cheese and the bottom of a four pound loaf accompanied by some raw onions as a savoury. But the most remarkable part of the meal had yet to come. Someone would call for a dozen eggs. These would be broken in the half finished mug of cider and consumed with relish under the eyes of admiring natives and astounded strangers". Eaten without "Haste, gluttony or greed ... His cutlery consisted of an old treasured pocket knife which he used with skill and dignity". Teapot himself was anxious to let it be known that he did not always eat like this for, in those days, agricultural wages were but 30 shillings a week. Jimmy Teapot was a man of many parts. As a boy he started as a wheelwright apprentice. Next, he was a cattle drover regaling us with the reason drovers carried an overcoat, even on the hottest summer day, to lay in a heap on a spot outside the gateway to divert the cattle into the right place: an old drovers' trick. Jimmy was famous for his bird-minding in the cherry orchards. He described it thus: "Get me 6 or 7 sheets of corrugated iron and some chains and fix 'em up in the best places in the orchard. Then I got to tie strings to the chains. When I comes to me of the strings I gives him a good pull and then another until them birds what's come to scrump the cherries be in such a mugglement they don't know whether they be a flying or a swimming". He walked the orchards from 4 am to 8 pm. He had a fine sense of humour. Gardiner illustrates this with the following tale, "Late one moonlight night I was taking him in my car from a broadcast and we passed a spot where an Elizabethan ghost is reputed to walk. I asked him if he had ever seen the ghost and he replied promptly "No, sir. She was afore my time".

Teapot finished his days in a cottage in the High Street, Chipping Campden. It was very touching to find the obituary of Jimmy Teapot and another favourite character, Mr George 'Shup' Hawkins in Gardiner's papers. 'Shup', as he was known locally in Ebrington where he lived, was a shepherd working for the Stanley family until he was into his eighties. He was playing cricket into his 70s.

## Local humour

Charles Gardiner held a talk in the Cheltenham Art Gallery on March 25th 1957. The correspondent reports "Roars of laughter filled the Cheltenham Art Gallery last night when stories in Cotswold dialect were told by Mr C Gardiner and Mr G Hart (George Hart, from the Chipping Campden silversmithing family) in the course of Mr Gardiner's lecture on Cotswold Humour and Dialect." Mr Gardiner pointed out that there were a number of distinct dialects which he illustrated with examples. He mentioned 'Tom Forrest' (Bob Arnold) of the *Archers* whose speech is typical of Burford and the South Eastern Cotswolds. The Chipping Campden dialect was 'the best of all'. The typical Cotswold humour of both North and South Cotswolds was to have a village of fools. "In the North Cotswolds it was Ebrington and the simple folk were called 'Yubberton Yawners'." One tale he regaled of the simple folk is: "the natives, jealous of the superior height of the neighbouring church tower at Chipping Campden, mucked their own church to make it grow. The manure placed round the foot of its walls caused the soil to sink and the local men rejoiced at this evidence that the building had growed smartish in the night." Then there were the Yubberton men who tried to hurdle in the cuckoo hoping to retain the bird and thus secure perpetual summer – others put pigs on the wall to

watch the band go by and one misguided farmer sawed a cart in half to make two carts while his neighbour whitewashed the bull in the hope of producing a white calf. This reputation was not always welcomed by the inhabitants of Ebrington. A young policeman on his first trip out to Ebrington from Chipping Campden made a comment about the fools of Yubberton to Bill Payne, a friend of Charles Gardiner and a well known local. The policeman was treated to the reply, "That's just where you be wrong, young man. 'Tis where all the fools come to!". To Gardiner this was the perfect Cotswold humorous rejoinder. From his collection of Cotswold humour he told of the sayings of the older folk "whose humour consisted of obstinacy, malapropism and often the quick answers. Mr Gardiner said, not that long ago he was told his house needed a coat of "that there 'emotion paint' " and he related the story (in his lecture) of the old man who was told by his doctor that he was suffering from too much nicotine and alcohol. When he went home, he told his wife that he had too much "of thar niobaccy and alcobeer". One countryman questioned on his alcoholic condition after a slight accident in his car, said that he had had "the best part of a smartish few", a fine example of shading a meaning impossible in standard English.

Gardiner concluded his talk with the hope that the true Cotswold humour would be around for many years to come.

## Newspaper articles

Between September 1958 and July 1960 C H Gardiner wrote a series of articles in the Evesham Journal with titles such as *Topical Tales, Cotswold Dialect, Birds, Beasts and Flowers, Links with Shakespeare* and many more fascinating subjects exploring all the information he had collected over the years on dialect and humour.

In the November 1959 article *Aspects of the Old Cotswold Dialect* he refers to Hugh Massingham's *Wold Without End,* a book set around Chipping Campden, published in 1932. He collaborated with H J Massingham at one time and so was an admirer of his work. In the December 1959 article, subtitled *Sound pictures,* he lists some of the onomatopoeic words that are still used in the Cotswold dialect such as 'quammocking', referring to the internal rumbling arising out of an upset stomach; 'chink', a colloquial name for the chaffinch mimicking its call; 'bobhowler' is a cock chafer beetle so called because when it is turned on its back it buzzes furiously – hence the Vale expression 'as drunk as a bobhowler'. It becomes self explanatory if you know what a bobhowler is and how it behaves when it loses its equilibrium. 'Knackle' is used to describe the noise made by the clicking of ill-fitting dentures. 'Cagnag' is a woman who nags. When Jimmy Teapot, a confirmed bachelor, was asked why he never married, he replied with a twinkle in his eyes, "Women? They be cagnags". "He snapped out the two syllables in a way which gave them a wealth of meaning", Gardiner wrote.

*Links with Shakespeare* (December 1959) gives words that still survive as 'mammet' meaning puppet or 'mommet' as still used for scarecrow; 'inchmeal' – bit-by-bit ; 'thriller' or 'filler' is the name given to the shaft-horse in a team as in Shakespeare's day. When four horses were ploughing single on heavy land on the Cotswolds before being superseded by tractors, they were described in this order: 'the foremost, in-the-lash, the body-hoss and the filler.' The *Going Going* article explains yet more words such as 'blizzy – nothing to do with a blizzard, but used in connection with a fire out of control as on a thatch roof.; 'one-armed sailor' for a pump; and 'zany' for simple."

In the January 1960 article *Where do these come from?* CHG tells a fine story about an impending trip planned to Coventry to see the Godiva Pageant.

Two elderly natives are on their allotment in a North Cotswold village overlooking the Warwickshire plain.

"Going to the pageant a Satudy, Tom?" asked Sam.

"No. I think not, " was the reply. "I reckon I'll stay at home and get my taters up."

"Ah! But you ought to go, Tom", his friend urged. "There'll be a master procession, a capital good fireworks display and what not. And you can ride in that their big motor as comfortable as a biddy."

Tom was still unimpressed. "No; we got to make the most of the weather, and I wants these yur taters home and dry".

Sam made his final appeal earnestly and confidentially, "But you don't know what you'm missing, Tom. There's going to be a naked 'ooman on a white hoss!"

Tom drove his fork into the ground after the manner of allotment holders declaring seriously, "In that case I shall go – I ain't sin a white hoss this long time."

"Dialect produces words and expressions with colour and shades of meaning often absent or unattainable in Standard English ... I have always been firmly of the opinion that nobody can speak the authentic dialect of a particular locality unless he has heard it or learnt it either as a native or during the young formative years. We have seen grow up, since the introduction of radio, a synthetic form of dialect known in the BBC as 'Loamshire' which cannot be assigned to any particular county or district and is sometimes called 'Cornish cockney'. I call to mind listening to an Upper Slocombe comedy of mine being broadcast. Much of it was in the Cotswold dialect. An actor of national repute in relation to dialects had been included in the cast. From a dramatic point of view his performance was faultless but he was hopelessly out of touch alongside the Cotswold natives with their authentic voices – I realized once again that there can be few dialects more difficult than the Cotswold. It has its equal in this respect however in the dialect of old Evesham and particularly Bengeworth ... Although I have resided in the Vale of Evesham for over 30 years, I've never attempted to imitate the local dialect and listening to Ben Judd how wise I was..." (Ben Judd was the *Evesham Journal* dialect correspondent who gave talks on this.)

### A man of many parts

Mr Gardiner's one pleasure pursuit was as a member of Broadway Golf Club for many years.

In 1966 *The Evesham Journal* announced – "Mr Charles Gardiner of Aldington, Evesham, gets the MBE in the New Years Honours. The award is presumably awarded in recognition of his distinguished service, since 1928, as Clerk of the Evesham RDC. But Mr Gardiner is a man of many parts. As an interpreter of country life and a teller of country tales, he has few equals, if any. His *Upper Slocombe* series of rural comedies broadcast by the BBC offered an authentic voice of the countryside and set a pattern which many other authors are still following. He is one of a few writers whose comments on the rural scene are not only appreciated by town dwellers but are accepted by countrymen as well."

"He has written and lectured extensively on the dialects of the Cotswolds and the Vale of Evesham: and, with unassailable authority, on regional and local history. He has collected and sung the half-forgotten folk songs of the region."

"The Evesham custom of land tenure by which tenants of market-garden land are able to deal direct with their successors over the settlement of in-goings, is one of the many specifically local subjects requiring legal and historical scholarship on which Mr Gardiner is the foremost authority."

"Under Mr Gardiner's administration, the Evesham RDC enjoys a pre-eminence for rural local Government. At the opening of the meeting of the Evesham RDC's Public Health committee meeting, on Monday, Mr Sydney Byrd, Chairman of the Council, conveyed the congratulations to Mr Gardiner on his award ."

"Mr Gardiner had not only served the community well for many years as clerk of the council but he had carried out valuable work in other public fields. His ready wit and good humour had often resolved a difficult situation in the council chamber. In sending his apologies for absence at the meeting, Mr W A Ewins, the Father of the Council, wished to add his congratulations and to remind the council that he was the only remaining member who was present when Mr Gardiner was appointed as clerk 37 years ago."

Charlie Gardiner ended his days in Aldington. His wife, Miriam, died in July 1966 only a month before he took early retirement as RDC Clerk due to ill health. They were married for 40 years. Sadly, on September 16th 1966, he died. His last engagement locally was to present the prizes at the annual Badsey Flower Show. There was a private funeral in Cheltenham with a public Memorial Service in St James Church, Badsey.

The obituary in the *Evesham Journal* concluded with the words: "... he kept clear of party political circles, counting his friends among all shades of opinion and being implicitly trusted by them all. He was undoubtedly a great man."

## Notes

1   *Your Village and Mine* by C H Gardiner, 1943, Faber and Faber. Other examples of Gardiner's writing are from articles he wrote for the Evesham Standard between 1959 and 1966. Other papers are in the Worcestershire Record Office, in particular MMS BA10879/201-4.

2   Charles Henry Gardiner was born on 12th February 1902 at 16 Bath Road Terrace, Rodborough, Gloucestershire. He was the first child born to Gilbert, a journeyman tailor and Mimosa Gardiner, née Butcher, a cook. Charles' grandfather, George Gardiner, was a blacksmith but by 1901 he was described as a 'boiler and engine fitter', married to Martha. Charles's father, Gilbert, came from a large family of five brothers and three sisters. Charles married Miriam Ewart in Bristol in 1925. Miriam was born in Berwick-on-Tweed, Northumberland in 1900. In the 1901 census her father was given as Joseph, a commercial clerk along with his wife Jane and two daughters, Mary and Miriam. Charles and Miriam's only child, a daughter, Mimosa Miriam was born in Berwick in 1925.

3   Arthur Savory farmed the Manor Farm in Aldington from 1873 to 1901. He wrote the book *Grain and Chaff from an English Manor.* Published in 1920, this is a classic description of English village life.

4   See also the chapter on *Council Housing* in this book.

5   John Henry Bird 1904 - 1981 was born and buried at Badsey.

6   See also *The Old Cotswold Dialect: selected articles by Charles Gardiner,* Vale of Evesham Historical Society, 2008. Available from the Almonry Heritage Centre, Evesham.

## Acknowledgements

Grateful thanks for their assistance to the staff at the Worcestershire Record Office, the Evesham Library, the Campden and District Historical and Archaeological Society, and the Registrar for the Stroud District in Gloucestershire. I am also grateful to Lionel Knight and Michael Barnard.

*A corner "Somewhere in England" June 1940*

*Dunkirk Lads - HOME -*

Michael Barnard's picture depicts a memory he has of when he was a pupil at Badsey School. It was the summer of 1940. Badsey was overrun by British servicemen who had been moved inland following their evacuation from Dunkirk. They stayed in the village for about three weeks until they could be assessed and returned to their own regiments. The picture shows the Stone House (now Badsey Hall), and some of the hundreds of troops. The barn to the left of the picture belonged to Mr Arthur Jones who lived at the Stone House.

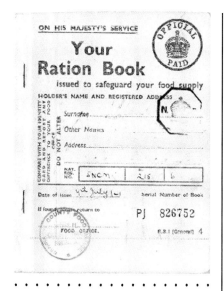

*Ministry of Food Ration Book from 1941.*

# 8

# THE VILLAGES AT WAR

## TONY JERRAM

*Tony Jerram was working on this chapter shortly before he died. He interviewed four local people about how the Second World War affected their lives. It was his intention to interview more. The final section is Terry Sparrow's memories of this time in his own words.*

Although it is now almost 70 years since the Second World War began, vivid memories are still held by those who lived through what were years of adventure and tragedy for some, and hardship and shortages for all. Things that were taken for granted then would seem incredible to many today. The blackout, ration books, utility china, barrage balloons, troop trains, powdered egg, clothing coupons, air raid shelters, Mr Chad and hundreds of other phrases have all slowly dropped out of everyday vocabulary.

Badsey was fortunate in being less affected by the war than many other places. Its rural situation meant that it was not a target for enemy bombers. The fact that many of the men in the village were engaged in food production as market gardeners meant they could enjoy the status of "reserved occupation" and, as such, were exempted from compulsory military service; basic food was not as scarce as it was in urban Britain. But the war touched all aspects of life, and brought massive changes to people in both town and country, so much so that certain events remain heavily scored in the minds of individuals. In this chapter, present residents of Badsey record some of their memories of the time when Britain was fighting, literally, for survival.

## A Misty Morning

Amongst the more persistent of Badsey wartime memories is the presence of probably hundreds of soldiers billeted in barns and houses in the village during the summer of 1940, in the aftermath of the evacuation from Dunkirk. A local military structure was soon introduced, which saw the Headquarters set up in Brewers Lane, a guardroom in the former cottage (now replaced by "The Rock") next to Malvern House, a canteen in the old school (now the Royal British Legion Club) and the troops' cookhouse in the block behind the Wheatsheaf Inn. One of those soldiers returned to the village after the war, and remains here still: he is 90 years-old Glanville Williams, who lives in Green Leys.

Born in Cornwall, and already a driver in civil life, Glan reported to the Royal Army Service Corps (RASC) barracks at Aldershot on 14th March 1940. After basic training he volunteered for a Mechanic's course, and duly qualified as an army Driver/Mechanic: "Not a sensible thing to do" he says: "as a driver/mechanic you were always the rearmost vehicle in the convoy, and had to round up stragglers. That meant that you were usually late arriving at your destination, and often missed out on meals."

In the summer of 1940, Glan was posted to an RASC unit based at South Littleton. After about three weeks there he was sent to a billet in Badsey, in Marshall's barn, close to the present Manorside and, after a few days, his eye was caught by Muriel,

the daughter of market gardener Arthur Taylor of Synehurst. However, towards the end of September Glan and his companions marched in full kit to Littleton and Badsey station and entrained for Liverpool to embark on the troopship Duke of York, which sailed for the Middle East on 6th October. The soldiers aboard called their ship the "Drunken Duchess" because she rolled so violently during the six-week voyage to Egypt via the Cape of Good Hope.

By late November Glan was with 922 Company RASC in Tobruk, and was destined to see four Christmases come and go in North Africa, as he was to stay on supporting the Sudan Defence Force in Cyrenaica after Rommel had been beaten and the British had gone. But his most dramatic experience came in 1942; on 9th June his unit left on a four-day operation to take part in the miraculous escape of the Free French brigade from Bir Hacheim. After two days of zig-zagging through the desert, the British vehicles laagered up at the rendezvous point a few thousand yards from the French "box". That night a rare meteorological event occurred – a mist descended on the desert and, at dawn, hidden beneath it, Glan and the others could hear the enemy planes overhead; they knew the vehicles were in the area and were seeking in vain to destroy them. Eventually, at 8am on 11th June, with his lorry full of French soldiers, all weary and some bloodstained, Glan was able to speed away. To this day, he says: "I felt that night at Bir

*Glanville Williams in North Africa.*

Hacheim that someone was watching over me." That heroic 16-day rearguard stand by the Free French allowed the British forces time to regroup, and thus to begin the long journey resulting, eventually, in the El Alamein offensive. And Glan? He was demobbed in July 1946, and returned to Badsey to marry Muriel, the girl who had been in his thoughts for nearly six years in, and beyond, the Western Desert.

## The Cruel Sea

In September 1939 Mike Hewlett would have his twelfth birthday. He was living in Synehurst with his parents, two brothers and a sister. His father, Ivor, had seen service in the Royal Navy in the 1914-18 war and had remained on the Fleet Reserve, which meant annual trips to Chatham for refresher training. When the Munich crisis had developed in the late summer of 1938 Mike's father, like many other reservists, had been briefly recalled to the Fleet for full-time service, only to be stood down as international tension eased. However, a second recall came in August a year later, as the storm clouds gathered, and a fortnight after the declaration of war Mike would celebrate his birthday at home without father.

As a trained reservist, Ivor was quickly posted to the crew of the fast light cruiser, HMS Enterprise. In October 1939 Enterprise, her sister ship HMS Emerald and two other vessels received orders to stand by for a top secret mission, and were told to report to Plymouth. On arrival there elaborate decoy measures were employed, including the ostentatious issue of tropical kit to the crews. However, the real purpose of the operation was to transfer the UK's stock of gold bullion to a safe haven, well away from any hostilities. The ships were loaded with the gold under the tightest security, and before the end of the month set off across the North Atlantic for Halifax, Nova Scotia to discharge their cargo.

Shortly after the bullion run, Ivor was transferred to the light anti-aircraft cruiser HMS Curacoa, one of the ships destined to take part in the short-lived but disastrous Norwegian campaign of April 1940. It was here, on 24th April, that she was hit just below the bridge by a bomb which killed 30 of her crew, injured another 30 and severely disabled her. She limped slowly homeward under her own steam

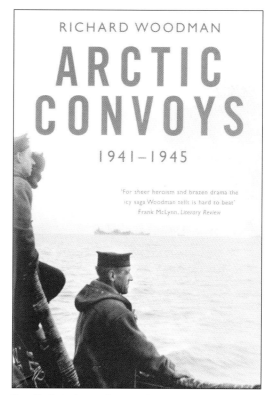

*Ivor Hewlett's photograph was used to illustrate the cover of the book 'Arctic Convoys' by Richard Woodman (John Murray, 1994).*

for 8 days, finally putting in to Chatham for repair and refit. While undergoing refit, half her crew at a time were able to take some home leave, and Ivor returned to Badsey to find it full of khaki-clad Dunkirk survivors. On his appearance in the village, wearing a sailor's uniform, the soldiers gave him a cheer and swept him off to the Wheatsheaf Inn in gratitude for the role played by the navy in getting them off the beaches.

Curacoa's repair and refit was completed by late July 1940, and after sea trials she took up convoy defence duties. Ivor had shore leave again in the winter of 1940-41, but while at home contracted severe influenza, which prevented his return to duty at the appointed time. After the environment which he had had to endure, often at battle stations aboard light cruisers operating in northern waters, it was not surprising that someone of his age should succumb to bronchial problems, and the illness eventually resulted in his being medically discharged from the service in 1941. With hindsight, his illness was a personal blessing in disguise for the whole Hewlett family because, on 2nd October of the next year, 1942, HMS Curacoa was sliced in half by RMS Queen Mary as both ships were manoeuvring to avoid U-boats. Because of the proximity of the enemy it was too risky for Queen Mary to stop to pick up survivors and, tragically, Curacoa sank with the loss of over 300 lives.

## BBC Home Service

In September 1939 Helen, the daughter of Nellie and Elgar Hartwell, one of the village butchers, was working in David Greig's, the grocer, in Bridge Street in Evesham. The Hartwell family had recently moved from an old cottage opposite the Wheatsheaf Inn to Hollywood Villa, further up the High Street. To this day the older residents of Badsey remember with fondness the faggots produced by Elgar; according to Helen they were made from bread soaked in water, lights, a small amount of liver, off-cut fat from joints and a proprietary mix of herbs from a supplier in Manchester. They were made in batches of a thousand at a time, and were cooked in the baker's oven in Brewers Lane. Often a young George Keen would be paid fivepence to take them on their journey as they were wheeled between butcher and baker on a trolley

In late summer 1940 Helen left David Greig's and went to work for the BBC at Wood Norton, where she would stay until after VE Day. At this stage of the war, with invasion threatening, BBC Wood Norton had become of critical importance. It had acquired the role of transmitting emergency information to the nation if London should go off the air and by early 1940 had become one of the largest broadcasting centres in Europe. Helen's work was principally as a teleprinter operator, one of a team of three, but she also sometimes took turns on the telephone switchboard. Her base was in the main house at first, although later she moved to a prefabricated extension. To get to work she usually cycled into Evesham where she could catch a BBC bus. Sometimes she cycled the whole way. Although she did not usually work shifts, one Christmas she did volunteer to work on the switchboard to let a married colleague have more time at home over the holiday.

Until 1943 Wood Norton was also home to the BBC Monitoring Service, whose members listened in to foreign radio networks round the clock as part of national intelligence gathering. The monitors were housed in temporary huts in the grounds. Helen also remembers that for some time the Midland Light Orchestra was based there, as were many BBC announcers. Naturally enough there was a lot of coming and going of people, and amongst them were the Corporation's War Correspondents, who underwent training there.

As an important part of the BBC's (and Britain's) war effort Wood Norton was of considerable interest to the enemy. Helen remembers that the

*Farewell party of BBC staff at Wood Norton July 1945.*

alarm signal, given in the event of air attack or other emergency, was the playing of the tune "Teddy Bears' Picnic" over the loudspeaker system. The bombing of the greenhouses at Chadbury, only a few hundred yards from the site, was evidence, if any were needed, of enemy attention.

The composer Eric Coates also had a connection with the BBC at that time, and Helen has particular memories of one of his pieces called "Up Badsey Lane". Eventually, in July 1945, just a few weeks after VE Day, several members of the wartime staff, including Helen, were selected for transfer elsewhere. After a farewell party in the canteen they went their various ways, and Helen duly reported for duty at BBC Birmingham.

## Hostel and Hard Work

In May 1943, 16 year-old Beryl Bishop was a cinema usherette living in King's Heath, Birmingham. The twin youngest of a family of eight, her mother had died when she was only four. Now, as the war dragged on, many of her friends had joined the women's Forces, but she was still too young to do the same. Instead, she went into central Birmingham and, claiming to be older than she really was, enlisted in the Women's Land Army (WLA), putting down "Scottish Forestry" as her preference for employment. Shortly afterwards, and to the great surprise of her father (she had not told him what she had done), her uniform, including boots, socks, breeches, dungarees, aertex shirt, jersey, hat, badge and greatcoat was duly delivered to the family home.

Soon Beryl was amongst a group of girls put on a train and told they were going to Worcester, where, on arriving, they were met and loaded on to a lorry. It dropped ten of them off at Wickhamford Manor, the first detachment of WLA girls to move into the Manor, recently vacated for them by Mr Lees Milne. Beryl's bedroom had five double bunks in it, there was a cook to prepare breakfast, packed lunches and tea for the girls, and a foreman overseer who gave them their orders and paid them their wages. Each girl was issued with a bicycle. For Beryl's first job she was sent to a farm in Bretforton to sort mangolds, but other tasks soon followed. Days were long, with a 5.30am call followed by breakfast and a cycle-ride to work for a 7.30 start. When the journey was as far away as Chipping Campden, a

*Beryl in her WLA uniform. She was a land girl from 1943 to 1945.*

lorry took them. Sometimes the girls had to return to work after tea. Within a short time they were all sunburnt and blistered: the hobnailed Land Army boots were merciless on their feet. In time more girls arrived at the Manor, increasing the number in residence to 25 or more.

Among the many jobs that came Beryl's way were haymaking, potato picking, fruit picking, topping beans and even driving sheep. However, she soon became a regular worker at Mr P J Simms' farm at Childswickham and was happy to have found in him a kind, generous and understanding employer.

Off duty, the girls found it easy to enjoy themselves. Trips to the YMCA in Evesham were popular, where they could relax over a cup of tea and a sandwich. Many evenings were passed happily at the Sandys Arms, which was also favoured by American and Canadian servicemen from nearby bases. Dances were regularly held in surrounding villages, and even, on occasions, at Wickhamford Manor itself. Those girls whose families were reasonably close like Beryl's often went home for a brief weekend, as work stopped at noon on Saturdays. Sometimes Beryl would take a friend home with her; they would walk from Wickhamford along Cow Meadow, then up Mill Lane in Badsey to the Badsey "Pike" where the Birmingham bus stopped. On returning on Sunday Beryl either used the bus again or caught a train to Evesham.

By February 1945, and after two winters working outside in all weathers, Beryl was advised that her health was deteriorating, and it was not sensible, or practical, to continue. Although by then she had made many friends she had no choice but to leave the WLA, which she did at the end of the month. However, the future was not totally unpromising, as she had already met Bernard Redgewell, the young Badsey man who she was to marry two years later.

## Terry Sparrow's recollections

My memories of this time in Badsey are those of a schoolboy as I was only five years old when the war began.

As children, we did not take kindly to the sweet rationing. Sometimes when my brother Patrick and I went for our allocation from Ernest Jones' shop (where the Spar now is) there would be an odd number of toffees, so we cut the odd one in half.

One day we heard that a number of soldiers had arrived in the village and that afternoon I went the 'long way' to school and there they were, mostly sitting on the kerbside outside the main church gate, opposite the post office. Later, we learned that they were part of the army evacuated from Dunkirk.

We had soldiers stationed in Badsey for some time –they had a large hut erected in the old farm yard opposite the Stone House. I think that some, too, were billeted in the back room at the Wheatsheaf Inn. They also occupied a house in Brewers Lane, now number 29, as headquarters. Sometimes, when the soldiers drilled in the road outside the house, we would stand a few yards away and imitate them, perhaps using sticks as rifles, until being chased off by some irate sergeant. A voluntary canteen was organised; I believe it was held at the Old School.

Early in the war Dad joined the Local Defence Volunteers (they wore arm bands with LDV emblazoned on them). Later, when the force was re-named the Home Guard, Dad was soon issued with a proper uniform, a rifle and, in due course, five rounds of ammunition which was stored in our dining room cupboard. Sometimes, on Sunday mornings, we watched the Home Guard drilling in the school playground.

I remember the issue of gas masks– uncomfortable and smelly–which for a time we had to take with us to school each day. Anyone who forgot was sent back home to fetch it. The school windows were taped to reduce the amount of flying splinters of glass which would be caused by a bomb blast.

In 1943 we heard the sad news that Dad's cousin, Philip Sparrow, was a prisoner-of-war in Java. It

*Left: These accounts suggest that the voluntary canteen at Badsey did brisk business in 1940*

*Opposite: A second impression by Michael Barnard of the days after Dunkirk. The picture is looking south down Badsey High Street with the cider press on the left. The petrol pumps once stood outside Schumachs (18 High Street). On the right of the picture, the iron railings had recently been cut down for the war effort.*

was a terrible shock to his mother (my great aunt Rose) who had lost her husband during the 1914-18 War. Once or twice a postcard from Phil arrived, but no one knew what was really happening to him until he came home after the war.

We children made a small contribution to the war effort by collecting rose hips from the hedgerows and digging up dandelion roots on waste ground. I suppose there was some sort of medicinal use. I certainly remember taking dandelion roots to Arthur Sears' yard in Badsey Fields Lane and receiving a few pennies for them.

Sometimes we saw American troops passing through the village in their jeeps. They appeared to have an inexhaustible supply of sweets and they were certainly our friends when they threw packets to us as they drove past.

November the fifth bonfires were banned, as were fireworks, but I don't think we felt deprived; after all, it was the same for everyone.

Although our family has always been Church of England, my brother and I attended the Sunday School held in the back room of the Friends' Meeting House in Chapel Street. The building is now the Dance Studio. The Sunday School was supervised by the brothers Willie and Eddie

Churchill, two market gardeners who were well known to us, as they worked land very close to that of our father and grandfather at Badsey Field. At Christmas time we were awarded prizes—as far as I recall everyone who had attended regularly throughout the year received one—and there was also an annual party. The food was wholesome if somewhat basic, due to wartime shortages, but I particularly remember the 'doorstep' sandwiches, about two inches thick and usually filled with either jam or fish paste.

The market gardening labour force was supplemented in two ways during the war. The first was by the formation of the Women's Land Army, mostly city girls with little knowledge of horticultural work. I recall some, in their green jerseys, working opposite our house in Brewers Lane. And secondly, the prisoners of war; Italians and then Germans. They were easily recognisable by the coloured patches sewn on to their jackets. Another job done by the Italian POWs was cleaning out Badsey Brook.

### Acknowledgements

Grateful thanks to Glanville Williams, Mike Hewlett, Helen Stanton, Beryl Redgewell and Terry Sparrow for their stories.

*This picture of the Manor House was painted by John Bird in
1983. The house looks almost the same today. The lively
timber framing is a mixture of lozenge or diamond patterns with
S-scrolls. It has an unusual rotational symmetry: if you turn the
picture upside down most of the pattern remains the same.
Today the building is divided into two. No 6 High Street is on
the left of the picture (the south side). The smaller No 4 is on the
right of the picture (the north side).*

*Outbuildings on the north side of the house about 1900, from the Victoria History of the County of Worcester*[1].

# 9

# THE SEYNE HOUSE

## RICHARD PHILLIPS

Badsey Manor House, also known as the Seyne House, stands at the north end of the High Street. At first glance, it is an Elizabethan House. The black and white half timbering makes an unusual and striking pattern which is probably unique to this building. Most of the house does indeed date from the late Tudor period, but there are other things to notice when looking at the frontage from across the road. There are now two front doors. What was once one large house has become a pair of 'semis' – Nos 6 and 4 High Street.

Around the front door on the left is a square frame that once was open. It led into a passageway through the centre of the house, wide enough for a horse and cart to pass through. Looking upwards, the roof is not right for a Tudor House. The roof slopes down at each end, but a Tudor building is unlikely to have been built with a hipped roof like this.

Look down and you will notice that it is only the upper part of the house that is half timbered. The ground floor is built of stone. With most Tudor houses the ground floor is also half timbered. The stone walls suggest an earlier building upon which timber framing has been placed.

### The monks in the Seyne House

There is a tradition that Badsey Manor House is on the site of an earlier building belonging to Evesham Abbey. Pevsner[2] says "…on the site of the Seyne House, an early fourteenth century rest house of Evesham Abbey, … perhaps incorporating earlier masonry…".

Before looking at the connection between the modern Manor House and the monks' buildings, it is worthwhile to consider the ways in which the Benedictines at Evesham Abbey made use of Badsey. The village was about two miles away from the main abbey buildings. Little of Evesham Abbey remains today and so it is easy to forget that it was once one of the most important monasteries in England.

The Domesday survey in 1086 tells us that Badsey belonged to the abbey. Arable farming there was on a large enough scale to make use of eight ploughs. There were just under 800 acres in cultivation. About 1233, the Chronicles of Evesham Abbey[3] tell us Abbot Thomas de Marleberge "caused certain pieces of land at Badsey to be cultivated, to the extent of five acres, which had never before been cultivated as long as men could remember." As well as being a religious body, the abbey was a large and successful business looking for ways to expand. Much of the abbey's income was from rents. But the monks found Badsey useful for more than just agriculture.

The Chronicles tell us that about 1317 Abbot Chiriton acquired a house and land at Badsey. About 1330 income was given to the abbey chamberlain "so that if either minuti or their fellow-monks of this abbey wanted to eat there, (permission having been obtained from the prior or his deputy), they should receive the corrody belonging to them (from both the cellar and the kitchen) just as fully as they would have if they were staying and eating at the abbey." The site at Badsey was therefore important enough to have its own kitchen. We are told it provided a catering service similar to that offered in the main abbey. The Chronicles mention nowhere else outside Evesham offering this special facility.

So what were the monks doing at Badsey? The clue comes from the Latin word 'minuti' which can perhaps be translated as 'the diminished ones'. Minuti were monks who had been bled, not because they were ill, but because it was part of the monastic ritual. The practice is so odd that it needs some explanation.

Blood letting seems to have been practised in most monastic communities. The 'Cistercian Usages' tell us in some detail what happened to their monks[4]. All were bled four times a year.

Recovery could take some days because several pints of blood were removed and the process continued until a monk was on the point of unconsciousness. Monks stayed in a heated room, had special food, and enough time to recover before returning to their normal work and duties.

For many centuries it was thought that bleeding could cure a wide range of ailments. But why bleed healthy individuals? A medieval manual claimed that the process "strengthens the memory, dries up the brain, sharpens the hearing ... produces a musical voice" among other supposed benefits. Some modern commentators have suggested that bleeding was done principally as a preventative against sexual arousal. Monks were supposed to abstain from any kind of sexual activity.

On the main abbey site at Evesham there was an infirmary to care for old and sick monks. It is likely that Badsey also carried out some of this work. In 1334 the Chronicles mention "a messuage with a garden and virgate of land in Badsey for the refreshment of the monks in sickness." The distant location may have partly been chosen to avoid contagion. Black death arrived in Europe in the 1340s. But a site away from the bustle of the abbey may also have been well suited for monks recovering from their ordeal of bleeding.

Two entries in the Chronicles mention improving conditions for monks who had been bled at Badsey. About 1362 money was provided "...to give and distribute a few pence from this sum to each individual monk who was bled, ... He should give the prior twice as much of the said sum, when he was bled. To retain the health of the healthy, and to relieve the infirmity of the sick; he freely added and granted two more days of rest to the aforesaid minuti... for they had formerly had no more than three days. ... he also granted single loaves of this type known as treycatm to every monk bled".

About 1400 an order was given to provide "three cartloads of straw a year, for the beds of the monks and the minuti" at Badsey.

Thus we know at least four monastic activities took place at Badsey: the abbey received income from agriculture there; it provided a catering service comparable to that at Evesham; it cared for sick monks; and it bled large numbers of healthy ones. Where did this happen? It is possible that more

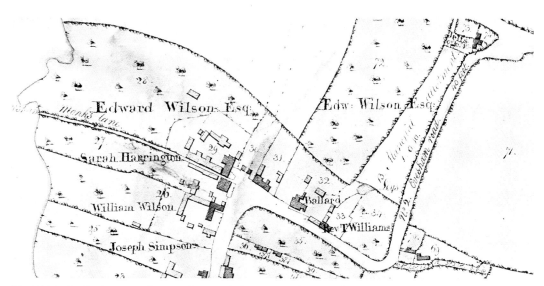

*The 1812 Badsey Enclosure map shows Monks Lane which is now the public footpath called Monks Path. It is a beeline to Evesham Abbey and must have been well trodden in medieval times. The Manor House and its outbuildings lie to the north of this path. Several other old buildings are close by including Harrington House, Oakleigh House and Oakleigh Cottage. This is the earliest map we have of Badsey and we can only guess what was here in medieval times.*

than one building was needed. There were perhaps a cluster of monastic buildings at Badsey.

Running along the south side of the Manor House is Monks Path, a public footpath that heads straight to Evesham Abbey. Tradition has it that this was the route used by the monks. We have no map or drawing of what the monks' buildings looked like. We can guess that they followed a simple medieval style – a single storey, built of stone with a wooden frame roof covered with thatch. When a fire was needed, it would have been on a hearth in the centre of the room. Unlike the more important abbey buildings in Evesham, it is unlikely that the stone was carved. It was probably the locally available lias rubble that is part of so many local buildings.

It made sense to reuse well-built walls and it is likely that some of these medieval walls found their way into the Manor House. One reason for supposing this, is that the Manor House is only half timbered from the first floor upwards. With most Elizabethan buildings, the half timbering starts just above ground level. But here, we guess, there were walls worth reusing.

Two walls which are likely to date back to the monks' time are on the west and south side of the north wing. They are about 600 mm thick – comparable in thickness to the medieval walls in the Almonry in Evesham[5]. In the west wall are two small high windows with splayed sides: dating them is difficult but the style is certainly medieval.

The Manor House has an alternative name: the Seyne House. It is this name that perhaps provides the strongest evidence of a link between the modern house and one of the monastic buildings.

### What is a Seyne House?

There is a written reference to 'a Seyne House in Badsey parish' in 1545 when Henry VIII granted it to Philip Hoby. The name seems to have stuck and today it still appears on a notice by the front doors. The monks may also have called it the 'Seyne House'. But what does the name mean?

Along with other 20th century writers, Arthur Savory[6] speculates that the word 'seyne' means 'health' and has a similar derivation and meaning to the word 'sanatorium'. It was a house for convalescent monks.

Although this explanation is appealing, it is not supported by the Oxford English Dictionary. The dictionary lists the word 'seyny' from the French word 'seigne' meaning 'bled'. Lewis's Middle English Dictionary[7] lists the same word with several spellings and several related meanings: "blood letting in a monastery, periods of leave from the usual monastic regimen for monks or nuns undergoing bloodletting, … a room, building, or part of a building set apart for ailing monks and those undergoing bloodletting, where the strict monastic diet was relaxed." This meaning closely matches our understanding of what the monks did at Badsey. So a seyny or seyne house would have been a house where monks were bled and recuperated.

Today 'seyne' is usually pronounced either as 'sane' or as 'sign' but it is possible that the original pronunciation was 'sane -y'. Old spellings are confusing but several suggest this possibility, for example a 1621 document mentioning the 'Seyney Howse in Badsey'.

## The Hobys

On 30 January 1540 the monks of Evesham Abbey were celebrating vespers. The commissioners appointed by Henry VIII arrived during the service, which they halted and, at the same moment, brought to an end 800 years of monastic history. The wealth of Evesham Abbey was claimed by the crown. It was divided up and sold or given away to friends of the king.

Like every community in the Vale, the people of Badsey must have been deeply affected by this change. The monks had various kinds of possessions in Badsey. They owned land and buildings. But they also had income from tithes. They owned the title to the manor of Badsey and the right to appoint the vicar. At the dissolution, these different types of wealth were not kept together in a tidy package, but split up and owned by different people[8].

One man who gained from the spoils of Evesham Abbey was Sir Philip Hoby. Coming from a Leominster family, he won the favour of Henry VIII by supporting the protestant reformation. He was sent as a diplomat to Spain, Portugal and Flanders and became a powerful political figure. Court papers for 1545 tell us that the king granted Philip Hoby property taken from Evesham Abbey for a fee of £888 16s 10d. This included the "Seynehouse, in Badsey parish, in tenure of the said Sir Philip; and two parcels of land lately enclosed outside Shrawnell park in Badesey parish, lately in the abbot of Evesham's own hands". Shrawnell Park is the area we now call The Parks. At some

*Above: The diplomat Sir Philip Hoby (1505 -1558) who acquired the Seyne House from Henry VIII.*
*Below: Philip's half brother, Richard Hoby, from the memorial in Badsey church. The memorial is misleading as it suggests Richard had no children of his own. His first wife and daughter, both called Elizabeth, are absent from the memorial. The memorial was erected by Richard's step daughter Margaret Delabere who remembered to include herself in the memorial as a child. Later she commissioned an even grander memorial in Bishops Cleeve church with effigies of herself and her late husband Richard Delabere.*

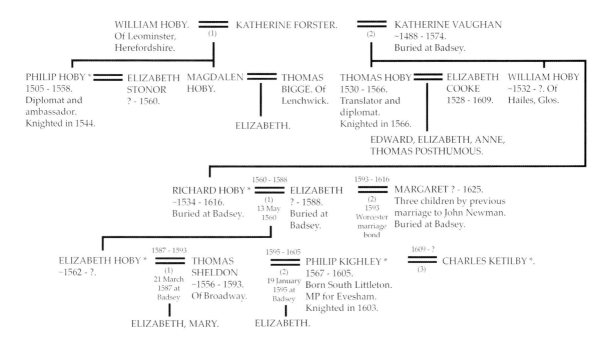

*A Hoby family tree. Owners of the Seyne House (marked \*) were: Philip Hoby, his half brother Richard Hoby, Richard's daughter Elizabeth with her second and third husbands.*

date after this, Philip Hoby gave the Seyne House to his half brother Richard Hoby, who was about 30 years his younger.

By the time Philip died in 1558 his wealth was considerable, a small part of which included land and tithes in Badsey and Aldington. His will passed these other Badsey possessions on to his half brother Richard. The 1558 will states "…my brother Richard Hoby shall during his life have the profits and occupation and use of the parsonage and tithes of Badsey, Wickamford and Nawnton … ". He was also given cattle, two of Philip's beer cups, wall hangings and "one half of my household stuff at Evesham".[9]

Philip's will makes it clear that Richard Hoby was living in Badsey at this time and Richard maintained close connections with the village until his death. He may have also lived for a period at Elmley Castle but there is a string of events that connect him with Badsey. In 1574 his mother Katherine was buried at Badsey. His daughter Elizabeth married there in 1587 and the following year his first wife was buried at Badsey. Richard Hoby was part of the Badsey community: he was a churchwarden four times.

When Richard Hoby first came to Badsey the Seyne House may have changed little from the monks' time[10]. But in 1587 major building work turned it into an impressive Elizabethan house. We know the date with some certainty from tree ring dating[11]. The timbers used to build the new house were mostly cut down in the winter of 1586/87 and it would have been the usual practice at that time to build during the following summer. 1587 is the same year that Richard's daughter married at Badsey church. The Spanish Armada attacked England a year later in 1588.

## The Elizabethan house

Above the ground floor, the house is built using a method of timber-framed construction that was popular and fashionable in Elizabethan times. The frames were made of oak and elm beams held together with wooden pegs. A series of cross frames run from the front to the back of the house dividing it into bays. More frames form the side walls, the roof and the individual rooms.

*Left and below: Some features in the house which date from Elizabethan times, or soon after: a cockshead door hinge, wood carving, and a stone fireplace in an oak panelled room decorated with arcading.*

*Right: The drawing shows one of the cross frames in the north wing of the house resting on stone walls. Oak and elm timbers were sawn or split into beams. These were assembled flat on the ground using wooden pegs. The house has a series of parallel cross frames like this. At the front of the house are three wider frames dividing the front into two bays. The north wing has two more frames (including the one illustrated) adding two more bays. The longer south wing has a further five frames and so five more bays.*

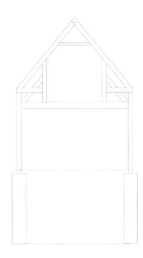

*No known picture survives of the Elizabethan house. This reconstruction drawn by the artist Ian Gibson is based on a mixture of research and guesswork. It shows the house soon after it was built in 1587.*

*We can be fairly certain that the front of the house had gables in the roof and that there was a passageway wide enough for a cart to pass through. We are less certain about the windows and the decorative pattern on the gables. It is possible that there were only two gables, not three. The windows at first floor level have been changed several times. Clues on the front of the house suggest that there were originally three jettied windows as shown here.*

*The decorations shown on the gables are called quadrefoils. These appear on one of the gables at the rear of the house and so may also have been used on the front. The timbering pattern is quite similar to Little Moreton Hall in Shropshire which was built about the same time.*

*The roof has a pitch of 50 degrees which suggests it was designed to be covered with Cotswold stone tiles.*

The spaces between the frames were filled with panels made from wattle and daub. The wattle was usually thin pieces of oak and hazel woven like a basket. This was covered with a daub made from a mixture of clay and dung strengthened with straw or, in the case of the Badsey house, with hair. The completed panel was lime-washed. Over the years, many of the wattle and daub panels have been replaced and the white panels of the modern Manor House hide a variety of infill materials including brick, lias stone, 19th century laths and modern building blocks. Today we often think of Elizabethan houses with black timbers and white panels but these colours are largely a 20th century fashion. The oak timbers naturally weather to a silver grey colour. The panels were probably a pale greyish brown, like the colour still visible near the north chimney stack where a small area has escaped modern painting.

Following a plan that was common at that time, the house was built in two halves. The north side (the right hand side looking from the road) was the working part of the house including a large kitchen. A wide passageway separated this from the south side and provided some protection against fire spreading from the kitchen to the rest of the house. The larger south side was the higher status part of the house. Both sides had doors leading into the passageway. Food cooked in the kitchen was probably carried across this passageway and eaten in a hall on the south side. This passageway was wide enough for a horse and cart to pass through. It was a good practical arrangement giving protection from the rain while unloading.

The illustrations on the page 126 show several features of the house which date from Elizabethan times, or soon after.

**The Wilson family**

The Wilson family owned the Manor House for more than 200 years. They arrived in Badsey after the Civil War and may have been one of the families who made their fortune from that conflict. An abstract of title[12] shows that in 1677 Nathaniel, Katherine and Thomas Smith made an agreement with Thomas Wilson which gave him their 1000 year lease on the Manor House[13], the title and rights of Lord of the Manor, and other land including Badsey churchyard.

The Wilson's first appearance in the Badsey parish records was in 1663 when Edward Wilson, son of Thomas and Catherine, was baptised. Two remarkable things about the Wilson family are their fondness for the name Edward and the number of wives they married. The descendants of Thomas Wilson were:

Edward Wilson 1663 – 1749 (1 wife)
Edward Wilson 1691 – 1737 (3 wives)
Edward Wilson 1720 – 1761 (1 wife)
Edward Wilson 1748 – 1797 (3 wives)
Edward Wilson 1793 – 1837 (1 wife)
Edward Wilson 1820 – 1907 (4 wives)

All these men owned the Manor House or lived there for at least part of their lives. Although one cannot speak for their wives, it is safe to say that these Edwards were comfortably off, buying and selling land, and pulling in income from rents.

Many of the Wilsons were buried in the chancel of Badsey church. The first Edward has this poem on his burial ledger:

This Earrly place and house of Clay being them dissolved
And pass away. Wee have A Building Firmer Stands
Than any house that made with hands. Serve God live just.
Do not delay. Such Blessed Mansion you'll enjoy.

Around 1800 the Wilsons made a number of changes to the Manor House. The family must have decided that an Elizabethan half-timbered house looked old fashioned and that a Georgian frontage would look better. The front of the house was totally altered and these changes remained until about 1910. They can be seen in a photograph on the opposite page. The oak timbers were covered with a render. The passageway through the middle of the house was filled in and became a bay window. The whole of the front of the roof was remodelled. The Tudor gables disappeared and were replaced by a much simpler hipped roof.

This change is evident from crawling along the roof space of the north wing. At the rear of the house there are neatly made Tudor timbers with

*Above: Timbers supporting the Cotswold stone tile roof. The builders' marks on the timbers are clearly visible.*

*Below: How the shape of the roof may have changed. The Elizabethan house is shown on the left and the modern house on the right.*

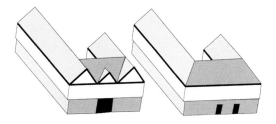

Roman numbers cut into them: I, II, III … counting from the back. About half way along, the numbering stops and the workmanship is noticeably poorer. Outside, the appearance of the roof is quite different at the front and the back: the Tudor gables are still there at the rear.

About the same time, the Wilsons built a small extension on the NE corner of the house. This made space for a new room, quite unlike any other in the house. Its pine panelling was once covered in gesso: a hard plaster made from chalk and coloured a grey green. Snowshill Manor has similar panelling where the gesso has survived, possibly by the same craftsman. In Edwardian times this was called the House Keeper's Room, and today, it is the front living room of 4 High Street. The staircases may also have been altered at this time. John Wingfield (of whom more later) tells us that there was once a chapel at the top of the house and that the last seats were said to have been removed by his grandfather about this time.

The Edward Wilson who was born in 1793 is interesting both for his role in the Badsey enclosures and also for his naval career. 'An Act of Parliament for Inclosing Lands in the Parish of Badsey' received royal assent in 1812. Its preamble includes these words:

> "And whereas Edward Wilson, an infant, is or claims to be Lord of the Manor of Badsey which comprises and extends over the whole of the said parish … "

Edward Wilson was in fact quite a large infant, being aged 18 at the time. His father had died in 1797 and there is no doubt that he inherited the right to be Lord of the Manor. The 1812 enclosure map shows he owned land in several parts of the parish. In the 1815 enclosure award, Edward Wilson owned 74 acres – the eighth largest landowner in the parish. The largest was Christ Church Oxford with 179 acres. Edward was certainly one of the winners from the Badsey Enclosure Act. Poorer people in the parish did less well.

Edward joined the 172nd Company of Royal Marines as a Second Lieutenant in 1813. We were at war with France. Napoleon surrendered in 1815 and was imprisoned on the remote South Atlantic island of St Helena. Lieutenant Wilson was a member of the garrison that guarded him there. Wilson describes Napoleon in his diary[14] –

"Height about 5 feet 5 inches, full face, particularly lower part, wide across his chest and

*The Georgian facade. About 1800 the Wilsons made major changes to the front of the house creating an appearance that was more fashionable at the time. This photograph was taken about 1900.*

shoulders, rather corpulent, legs rather large, hands beautifully small and delicate, and were much admired by a lady (who particularly noticed them). In conversation, to some, haughty and imperious..."

During his time in the navy Lieutenant Wilson travelled to Madras, Ceylon and the Cape of Good Hope. In 1825 he was appointed to the Portsmouth Division of the Royal Marines. By 1837 he had left the service and was home in Badsey. He became a churchwarden but died later that year aged 44.

After Lieutenant Edward's premature death, his widow Sarah wrote to the Admiralty in London for financial assistance. She was granted £10 pa for each of her three daughters Emily, Selina and Matilda, but her son, another Edward, aged 17 was too old to qualify. It is also likely that parts of the Manor House were let out. We know that in 1830 Mary Ballard made an agreement to rent part of the house and also the right to occupy the first pew

*The kitchen about 1912, looking through to the housekeeper's room. There is a cooking range in the fireplace and a telephone on the wall. It is likely that this room was used as a kitchen since Elizabethan times. The huge oak beam over the fireplace was felled in the year 1586. Today the room has become the living room for the north side of the house.*

in the chancel of the church. But the family's money problems continued. About 1850 they left Badsey and let the house and farm to William Parker who signed a 14 year lease in 1852. He came from Warwick and was a successful tenant farmer. By 1861 he was farming 120 acres and employing 8 labourers and a boy.

Sarah Wilson was buried at Badsey in 1857 and her son Edward decided to sell the house. The 1866 sale bill offered "All the messuage being the Old Manor House of Badsey, with the extensive farm buildings, gardens, yards, and valuable piece of pasture land or Cherry Orchard, thereto adjoining ... extending from the public road to Badsey Brook, containing with the sites of the buildings, 5a. 0r. 10p...". But the house did not find a buyer. However Edward did raise some money from the sale of land, including Badsey churchyard which was bought by the parish. Edward also sold his title of Lord of the Manor which was bought by Christ Church Oxford. But he continued to own the Manor House. By 1871 there was a different tenant, Joseph Jones, a farmer, and his family.

About 1873 Edward Wilson decided to return to Badsey Manor House. He had been the innkeeper of the New Inn at Longford St Catherine in Gloucestershire, and before that had been living in Cheltenham and Birmingham. Now he was returning home. In 1881 Edward and his third wife Ann were living in the house with one servant. Part of the house was occupied by tenants Herbert Kite and his family. Ann died in 1885 and in 1889 Edward married his fourth and last wife Emma Knight who was 32 years younger than he was.

The Parish Magazine for 1905 advertised the services of Nurse J Beesley, midwife and nurse, and gave her address as Manor House, Badsey. She was probably one of several tenants who lived alongside the Wilsons.

The Wilson family era came to an end with Edward's death in 1907. The parish magazine remembered him with affection "He was kindly and good-natured to a fault and, with his old-fashioned courtesy...".

Edward's only surviving son Edward Joseph Wilson put the Manor House on the market. He moved his family to a new home specially built for them: Cherry House at 83 Bretforton Road which stayed with the Wilson family until 1981.

*The rear of the house and some of its outbuildings photographed about 1912. The stone building on the left may have been stables with a hayloft above. It appears on the 1812 enclosure map and was demolished in the 1940s. John C Goom Architects used this as a source of inspiration for a new building built on the same site in 2008.*

## 20th century turmoil

The Badsey Parish magazine for December 1907 carried this news item:

> "We are pleased to note that the Manor House of Badsey, which was offered for sale on Monday, November 18th, has not been allowed to pass entirely out of the hands of the family who have owned it for over two centuries and a half. The property has been purchased by Mrs Wingfield (sister of the late Mr E Wilson) and her son, Mr J T Wingfield, of London. We look forward to the time when Mr Wingfield may possibly come into residence at the Manor House and take his part in the public life of the village which has been for so many generations the home of his ancestors."

John Tutin Wingfield of Stamford Hill, London bought the house and land for £880 and enthusiastically set about restoring it. His most dramatic change was to the front of the house changing it from a dull Georgian building back to something like its appearance in Tudor times. The following rough notes are from a talk that Wingfield gave in London.

> "Generation after generation had done its best to spoil it and it has been our lot, so far as is practicable to restore it to its original design. ...uncovered timbers (covered with plaster) on front. Our surprise (not to say delight). Gable ends at back of house plastered over. The oak in many cases in a wonderful state of preservation..."

The half timbering was exposed and could be seen for the first time in about a hundred years. The passageway between the two halves of the house was opened up again. However Wingfield's restoration did not include undoing the changes to the roof. This may have been because of the cost, or perhaps because he missed its importance.

We know about the extent of Wingfield's changes from a 'To Let' notice about 1909:

> "Considerable repairs are in course of execution... A dwarf wall of stone ... substituted for the iron railings ... entrance

*The house about 1912 after Wingfield had restored it to an Elizabethan appearance.*

gates will shortly be erected. The Kitchen Garden, Pasture Orchard and Paddock at present let on short tenancies… Outbuildings consist of stabling for 4 horses, harness room, loft, carriage or motor house, granary over coal house, cow house. Pleasure garden … croquet lawn has been laid out … provision for a full-sized tennis court... excellent spring water from a well, but if desired … willing to lay on water from the main … connection to sewer is laid. … Key from Mrs Wilson, Badsey House, Badsey.'

Wingfield brought with him a new set of attitudes about preserving old buildings. Thirty years before William Morris had held the inaugural meeting of the Society for the Protection of Ancient Buildings. The National Trust was founded in 1896. Without Wingfield's efforts it is unlikely that the house would be standing today.

Wingfield had some difficulty in finding the right tenant. He was still living in London himself and seemed to have given up any idea of moving to Badsey. Mrs Emma Wilson who was Edward's widow stayed on in the house until November 1910.

On 22 June 1911 a special event was held in the back garden to mark the coronation of George V. It was recorded in some memorable photographs[15] taken by the young Charles Binyon. Teachers and children from Badsey School joined by other residents took part in a pageant with maypole dancing and costumes representing countries of the British Empire.

In May 1912 Wingfield finally found a tenant for the house, although it may not have been quite what he had in mind. A clergyman from Birmingham, John Ludlow Lopes rented the house as a boys' home. A year later Lopes bought the house from Wingfield for £2250. Just before World War I Lopes established two homes for boys in the village. Younger boys were at Badsey Hall (the Stone

House) which Lopes renamed St Christophers. Older boys stayed at the Manor House which he called St Benedicts. The Stone House had a chapel and there were plans to build one at the Manor House. On 21 March 1914 a foundation-stone for the chapel was laid by Rev P H Brown, principal of St Stephen's House, Oxford. The stone inscribed in Latin is still in the garden of 6 High Street but the chapel was never built. Fifteen boys from the homes, aged from eight to 14, were enrolled at Badsey School. Many of them came from Birmingham and were remembered as quite a 'rough bunch' by other schoolchildren at that time.

It is unclear what events brought this project to an end. The outbreak of World War I in July 1914 was shortly followed by Lopes's decision to convert to Catholicism. He travelled to Rome in May 1915 where he was received into the church. The home closed in July 1915, the boys moved to another home at Pershore, and in October, Lopes sold the house and garden for £1300 to William Baker Driver who lived near Cirencester. Two fields to the north were sold separately: Synehurst and Brook Meadow. Synehurst field became the site of Badsey's first council housing and its first tenants moved in about five years later. At that time W Wilkins was tenant of the orchard land which stayed with the house.

The house was sold again in 1917 to George Mitchell Weekley, a London barrister for £1600. It is likely that both Driver and Weekley were investing in property and neither spent much time in Badsey. It was not long before Weekley had a tenant for the house but again it may not have been the one he wanted.

## German prisoners of war

During World War One there was a shortage of labour to work on the land. The Board of Agriculture and Fisheries set up a scheme 'Employment of German Prisoner Ploughmen'. German prisoners of war were moved to camps across the country to be available for work. There were about 23 camps in Worcestershire. The first prisoners arrived in the Evesham area in the summer of 1917. In February 1918 the *Evesham Journal* tells us 100 prisoners were moved to the Badsey Manor House making a total of 420 prisoners in the Evesham District with others at Hampton House and Craycombe.

The Badsey prisoners worked for local market gardeners. Some of the prisoners in Evesham were skilled basket makers. This skill was important for getting produce to market. Initially employers paid 4d per hour for the labour, of which the prisoner retained one penny. Correspondence in the *Evesham Journal* expressed concern that this was less than the going rate of pay and it was increased to 5d per hour to avoid a dispute about rate-cutting.

The German prisoners were based in the Manor House surrounded by a high fence. The soldiers who guarded them were billeted nearby in the Old School (now the British Legion) and their commandant, Lt Stubbs, stayed with the Sparrow family on Willersey Road.

Small groups of prisoners were sent off to work wherever they were needed. A relationship of trust began to build up between the market gardeners and the prisoners. There is a story of a market gardener in Badsey lending a prisoner a bicycle to ride over to a field at the other end of the village. One employer sent his small child to escort a prisoner to work.

For some the relationship between prisoners and locals was seen as too cosy. A writer in the *Evesham Journal* for 20 April 1918 expressed concern that he had seen 'young girls waving their hands and making overtures to the prisoners'. A farmer who had given his prisoners cider was deplored. Among the official papers, there is a stern enquiry about a farmer who allowed a prisoner to hold his gun.

In May 1918 there was some excitement when three prisoners from the Drill Hall Camp at Evesham escaped while working at Longdon Hill. A search party was organised and Harry Kelland, a Badsey man, came across the three taking a rest in a spinney near Wormington and recaptured them.

The Badsey Parish Magazine for December 1918 tells us about a prisoner who died – "The Vicar was present at the funeral of Private Rosskopf, the German soldier who was buried at Badsey on November 16. The deceased being a Roman Catholic, Monsignor Patten officiated. The grave is near to those of our own three soldiers, who have died within the last twelve months. The German soldiers from the Manor House Camp attended and, at the close of the ceremony, filed past the grave, each casting a handful of earth upon the coffin according to custom. There were some

*Denis Dickinson installed this piece of stained glass in the 1950s. Walther Von der Vogel Weide was a twelfth century minstrel who roamed across Europe and wrote in German. He adopted the image of a caged bird as a personal symbol. The imagery of a captured bird seems perfect for a house that was, for a short while, used as a prison.*

beautiful wreaths. Private Rosskopf came from Bavaria and leaves a widow and two children – RIP." The body of Johann Rosskopf was exhumed on 21 February 1963 and moved to a German cemetery at Cannock Chase.

There were still prisoners at Badsey in May 1919 but they must have gone home soon after this. Interviewed in 2001, Evelyn McKanan-Jones could still remember the prisoners. She recalled that security was low and that there was a hole in the perimeter fence in Monks Path. She and a school friend talked to the prisoners and they were sometimes given sweets to eat.

### Between the wars

The house had met the combined onslaught of teenage boys from Birmingham followed by German POWs. Whatever this did to the structure was made worse by a period of neglect over the following 25 years. However the house still continued to be used in a number of ways.

About 1928 the Manor House was used as a location for a feature film. The rear of the house became 'Ye Sweete Content Inn' for the film *The Price of Divorce* starring Wyndham Standing and Frances Day. It was a silent movie made in 1928 directed by Sinclair Hill, but was never completed. However it did see the light of day in 1930 when it was developed into a 'talkie' called *Such is the Law*. A 1927 film by the same director, *The King's Highway* may also have used the house as an exterior.

After the First World War the house was still owned by George Weekley. In 1936 he left it in his will to his daughter Edith Llewellyn Smith. Neither of these people appear to have lived in Badsey and they probably rented out what they could. Some parts of the house were derelict and in the 1930s it was not difficult for children to get inside and explore.

Mr D Wakefield[16] describes staying in the north side of the house during World War II: "We moved to Bretforton … and then Badsey village bakery before moving into the servants' half of a 14th century manor house that hadn't been occupied since it held German prisoners of war in 1919. The dark solitary confinement cell was upstairs with the regulations in German. The kitchen was stone flagged and some 40 x 15 feet while the door key was iron and weighed almost a kilo. It was unheated so we lived in the buttery (lined with copper to keep out the mice we were told). Sanitation was a bucket. 3 feet outside the back door was a wooden cover over a 4 foot diameter well..."

Towards the end of the war, the less derelict south side of the house was occupied by Maurice Harvey and his family. Mr Harvey had accompanied evacuee children from Birmingham in 1940, taught at Blackminster School and, in 1946, became acting headmaster of Badsey School. Maurice's son Richard recalls how he and his sister Pamela had free rein to play in both sides of the house and in the grounds which went right down to Badsey Brook. Richard remembers that a Mrs Stribblehill, who sometimes looked after the children, was

*Miriam Seegar and Wyndham Standing in the 1928 silent film 'The Price of Divorce'. The window is at the rear of the Manor House.*

convinced that the house was haunted. To appease her, the Harveys agreed to have the house exorcised by a Catholic priest, Father Proudman. The Harveys stayed for just over a year including one cold winter when it was impossible to get the house warm. Another occupant of the south side of the house was market gardener John Jones who moved to Taddington in 1944 to become a farmer.

## Harry Robinson

The next turn in the story came when Harry Robinson and his wife from Lancashire visited Badsey soon after the end of the Second World War. The Manor House must have been an appealing ruin. The chimney stack on the north side had collapsed, many windows were broken, and some rooms still had German notices from the First World War. Mrs Robinson persuaded her husband that they must restore the house and make it their home. This was no easy matter. Although the war was over, building materials were still in short supply. First they had to discover who owned the house and try to buy it.

The Robinsons made a temporary home at Claybrook Farm on the Bretforton Road. With some difficulty they contacted the owner and negotiated the purchase. On 31 May 1946, Lady Edith Smith, by then a widow living in Oxford, sold Harry Robinson the house and a sizeable area of land for £2,100. The Robinsons moved quickly and by the end of June, Henry W King, a surveyor from Evesham, had drawn up detailed plans to restore the building and convert it into two dwelling houses. The project was funded from the Robinsons' family coach business back in Lancashire.

The Robinsons' daughter Isabel recalls that the restoration was time consuming and difficult. The north side of the house (now 4 High Street) was in the worse condition. On that side an extension was built to make a kitchen. The chimney stack was rebuilt using the original stones. A parquet floor was laid in the old kitchen to make a living room. Wood panelling that had disappeared was replaced, carefully matching the original design.

The wide cobbled passageway that separated the two halves of the house was once again filled in, creating a space that became the entrance hall for the south side of the house (6 High Street). This was paved with stone slabs carefully removed from the living room on that side. Two entrance doors appeared on the front of the house. Two new staircases had to be built.

WITH THANKS TO ROY PAGE

By September 1947 the Robinsons were living in the larger house (No 6) and that month, the smaller house (No 4) was sold for £3,200 to Kenneth Johnson an Evesham solicitor. Almost all the changes made by the Robinsons remain to this day.

Harry Robinson ran several businesses from his side of the house which he called the 'Manor Dairy'. There was a retail dairy selling milk to the local community, a turkey farm, and orchards that extended from his garden down as far as Badsey Brook. Harry also tried his hand at mink farming. A small wooden sign saying 'Dairy' is still visible on the front of the house. David Caswell, the Badsey blacksmith, worked for Harry and remembers the family with affection, although there is no doubt that Harry was a shrewd businessman.

In 1949 the Robinsons sold a piece of land to the north of the house. A further piece was sold in 1950. It became a yard for Marshalls Transport, who also had premises at Aldington Mill. In 1987, Manorside was built on this site.

The house still had about 4 acres of orchard going down as far as Badsey Brook. In 1967 this was sold too and Manor Close was built on the site.

Harry Robinson remained in the house at 6 High Street until his death in 1970. His part of the house was then sold to Geoffrey and Vivienne Bowler who were both veterinary surgeons. Geoffrey had a handlebar moustache and was a familiar figure in the Wheatsheaf Inn. The Bowlers held a number of village fetes in their back garden, probably the first since the pageant of 1911. At the end of the garden was a paddock where ponies were kept. This was converted into a vineyard with 50 vines, producing wine for their own use.

In 1987 the Bowlers sold their house to a computer software business for offices, who in turn sold it to Lars and Anna Pegers. They were there from 1991 to 1999. Lars held a senior position in Swedish Steel. The present occupants are Dorothy and Alan Ayling, and May Watson.

Next door, at 4 High Street, Denis and Cecille Dickinson occupied the house with their family from 1953 to 1967. Denis, a research chemist, added much of the stained glass that is a feature of that side of the house. Their next home was a bungalow in Ireland which they named *Seyne Cottage*.

In 1967 Sonya and Michael Ealey moved in and their five children grew up in the house. Sonya represented Badsey as a councillor on Wychavon District Council and Michael was a civil engineer. During this time the Ealeys rediscovered the well on the north side of the house and partially excavated it. They also noticed that the 'house was bigger outside than inside' leading to the discovery of a large unused space, big enough to make an en suite bathroom.

In 2000 the Ealeys sold their house to Elizabeth Noyes and Richard Phillips (the writer of this chapter). Elizabeth laid out the front garden as a 16th century parterre with box hedges.

## The names of the house

We have already discussed the name 'Seyne House'. It is likely that this name was passed on to the field called Synehurst and so to the roads and housing estate with the same name. It is not surprising that such an old building should have picked up other names along the way. Two documents dated 1600 and 1677 called it 'Seneis' – perhaps meaning the 'house of the old man'. The 1677 document gives it an alternative name 'Cheney House' and this is also used in 1545. Both Seneis and Cheney sound like corruptions of Seyne.

The building is usually called Badsey Manor House. Although Richard Hoby owned the house for about 40 years he only held the title of Lord of the Manor for two years[8]. The Wilson family held the title for almost 200 years. They sold the title to Christ Church Oxford in 1866 who still remain Lord of the Manor in Badsey today, although they have never owned the house. It is clear that the ownership of the house and of the title have often followed separate paths. Despite this, the house continues to be called the Manor House. The name has stuck and it is the name that appears on Ordnance Survey maps.

More recent names for the house include St Benedicts (from Rev Lopes), 'Ye Sweete Content Inn' (as a film set), Manor Dairy (Harry Robinson's business), and simply Nos. 4 and 6 High Street.

## Undiscovered secrets?

Like many old buildings, Badsey Manor House has its fair share of stories about hidden treasure, underground cellars and secret tunnels. Sadly, there seems to be very little substance to them. Perhaps the most inventive – and the most unlikely – is an underground tunnel connecting the house to Evesham Abbey two and a half miles away. This highly improbable idea seemed to have motivated a group of amateur archaeologists called the 'Birmingham Enterprise Club'. In 1957 they were granted permission to excavate in the gardens by the two owners at that time. Their most interesting find "… in Mr Robinson's orchard 100 yards behind the house revealed a deep-laid primitive drain". When this drain was broken into, water spurted up from it, presumably because it had collected water from the higher ground nearer the house.

With almost seven centuries of history, the house may well have more secrets to reveal. But for this writer, there is more than enough to consider already.

## Notes

1  *Victoria History of the County of Worcester, Volume 2*, pp 353- 359, edited by J W Willis Bund and W Page, 1906.

2  *The Buildings of England: Worcestershire* by Alan Brooks and Nikolaus Pevsner, 2007.

3  *The Chronicles of Evesham Abbey: an English translation* by D C Cox, 1964.

4  The 'Cistercian Usages' are described in an article 'The English Cistercians and the practice of medicine' by D Bell, *Citeaux* 40, pp 139-173, 1989.

5  *The Almonry Museum, Evesham, Worcestershire*, The Vale of Evesham Historical Society, 1975.

6  *Grain and Chaff from an English Manor* by A H Savory, 1920.

7  *Middle English Dictionary* by Robert E Lewis, 1952.

8  This chapter is concerned with the ownership and occupation of the house. For more information on the title to the manor and the advowson see *A Brief History of Badsey and Aldington*, second edition, by T C Sparrow, Badsey Society, 2002.

9  In 1917 E A B Barnard wrote an article for the Badsey Parish Magazine about the will of Sir Philip Hoby. The article is reproduced on the Badsey website www.badsey.net

10  There is a possible reference to the house in the margin of the Badsey Churchwardens' accounts for 1552 and 1553. Next to an entry that says 'paid for the inventory' there is a note that says 'search the office in the siyeame'. The 'siyeame' is probably the Seyne House.

11  *Dendrochronological analysis of oak timbers from 4 High Street, Badsey, Worcestershire*. Tree-Ring Services Report EVHS/08/08 by A K Moir, 2008. Four timbers had precise felling dates in the winter of 1586/7 and another in the spring of 1586. It was only possible to date oak timbers as the analysis does not work with elm. Four other houses were surveyed at the same time: Harrington House in Badsey, and in Aldington, Manor Court, Elm Cottage and Rose Cottage. Unfortunately none of these could be dated because their timbers are nearly all elm. Elm seems to have been the preferred local building wood.

12  Worcestershire Record Office BA7842.

13  During the last years of Richard Hoby's life the ownership of the house appears to have been transferred to his daughter Elizabeth, and her second and third husbands, Philip Kighley and Charles Ketilby. In 1616 Charles and John Kettleby sold the freehold of the manor and lands to Sebastian Harvey. He was an ironmonger and a London alderman who in 1618 became Lord Mayor of London. A 1621 document says that Sebastian and his wife Mary owned 'a capital messuage called le Seyney Howse in Badsey'. Following his death, there was a long and expensive court case eventually settled in 1631 with the Badsey manor title and house going to Harvey's daughter and her husband John Popham. It passed to John's brother and heir, Alexander Popham (1605-1669). He was a politician and best known as patron of the philosopher John Locke.

In 1657 Alexander granted Nathaniel Smith a lease on the house, the manorial title and other property in Badsey for the term of 1000 years at the yearly rent of one pepper corn. Nathaniel died in 1677 and in the same year his heirs, Thomas, Katherine and Nathaniel Smith sold the same to Thomas Wilson. Before 1677 the house was occupied by Thomas Hassard, suggesting that the Wilson family were living elsewhere in Badsey. It is likely that most of the owners between the Hobys and the Wilsons were absentee landlords.

14  Edward Wilson's diary is in the Worcestershire Record Office together with other interesting papers from the Wilson family.

15  Two of the 1911 photographs are reproduced on page 115 of *A Brief History of Badsey and Aldington* (see note 8) and another two on page 67 of *Heads and Tales: a history of Badsey Schools* by Maureen Spinks, Badsey Society, 2004.

16  Wakefield's full story appeared on the BBC website in the series *WW2 People's War*, 2006. Ted Wheatley's memoirs tell us that the house was used by the troops returning from Dunkirk in 1940. See www.badsey.net

## Acknowledgements

Foremost, I would like to thank my partner Lizzie Noyes for many fascinating conversations about the house and its history. My son Will Phillips has helped us with our investigations. I am grateful to several former occupants of the house for information including Sonya and Michael Ealey, Cecille Dickinson, Isabel Mansell (née Robinson), and Vivienne Bowler, who has given the Badsey Society papers from her late husband Geoffrey Thomas Bowler. Maureen Spinks has helped in numerous ways including providing details of her work on the Wilson family. Among many others who have given valuable information and advice I would like to thank David Caswell, the late Tony Jerram, Ivor Martin, Roger Martin, Andy Moir, Roy Page, Mark Parsons, Fred Roberts and Terry Sparrow.

# SUBSCRIBERS TO THE BOOK

Pete & Ro Addis
George Aldrich
Mrs I Allen & Mr G E Allen
Mr & Mrs Michael J Barnard
Gillian Bartlett (née Redgewell)
Mrs W Beasley
Marianne & Chris Beddis
Adrian & Rosy Bennington
Mr & Mrs M B Bent
Mrs Janet Betteridge
John Bird
Rosemary Blyth
Elizabeth & Ralph Bolland
Louise Bufton
Mr & Mrs R Butler
David & June Caswell
Jane Charlwood
J & L Clarke
Martin, Karen, Hannah & Laura
    Coldicott
Mrs Susan Cole
Graham Corbett
Linda Core
Crane Family
Graham & Elizabeth Cudd
Richard Cudd
John & Will Dallimore
Susan Daniels
Ross Davis
Betty J Dennis
Alan & Mary Rose Eames
R M Ecroyd
Karen Evans (née Woodcock)
Les and Sharon Evans
Ian & Lynn Gibson
James Glover
Michael Green
Irene Grose-Hodge
Irene Guise
Graham & Christine Haines
Colin J Hall
John & Julie Hall & family
Mrs Peggy Hancock

Julia Harrold
Les Hartwell
Tony & Rosemary Hartwell
Betty Heath (née Smith)
A B Hewlett
Joan & Bernard Hewlett
Michael Hewlett
Gordon & Elaine Hill
Trevor & Beryl Hockenhull
David & Doreen Jack
Barbara Jerram
G R Keen
Dennis & Mary Knight
Mrs Jean Lavell
W T H & K P Lewis
Sandra Lovatt
Joyce Marshall
Ivor Martin
Roger Martin
Mike Neal
Robert Neill
Beth Norman
Gloria E Norman
Elizabeth Noyes
Michael A Overd
Christine Owens (née Redgewell)
Roy & Mary Page
Mrs Lesley Perry (née Badsey)
Arthur Plant
Jean Plummer
Brian Redgewell
Mrs Beryl Redgewell
Norman Redgewell
Evelyn Ritterswuerden
Arthur Ruff
Mr & Mrs A J Seller
Lynda & John Sharp
Kathryn Small
Brian & Hazel Smith
Pete & Liz Smith
Roy Smith
Miss S M M Smith, MBE
Mr V C E Smith

Ann Sparrow
Judy & Patrick Sparrow
Sandra Sparrow
Mrs Elizabeth Spencer
Tony, Maureen & Jonathan Spinks
H M Stanton
Craig Jonathan Stevens
Gill & Clive Stewart
Mr M Taylor
Susan Thompson
Robert A Thould
Howard & Phyllis Timms
Pat & Brian Tomkins
Steve, Kim, Connor, Alex &
    Claudia Trotman
Margaret & Irene Tyszkow
Brian & Camilla Watkins
Bert Weaver
Chris Winton
Ian Wolfenden
W H Wood
Ron & Bev Wyatt (Canada)

# INDEX